P9-DCW-623

10/04

SPRINGDALE PUBLIC LIBRARY
405 S. PLEASANT ST.
SPRINGDALE, AR 72764

TIME

Great Buildings Of the World

The World's Most Influential, Inspiring
And Astonishing Structures

_____

GREAT BUILDINGS OF THE WORLD

EDITOR	Kelly Knauer
DESIGNER	Ellen Fanning
PICTURE EDITOR	Patricia Cadley
WRITER/RESEARCH	Matthew McCann Fenton
COPY EDITOR	Bruce Christopher Carr

TIME INC. HOME ENTERTAINMENT

PRESIDENT	Rob Gursha
VICE PRESIDENT, NEW PRODUCT DEVELOPMENT	Richard Fraiman
EXECUTIVE DIRECTOR, MARKETING SERVICES	Carol Pittard
DIRECTOR, RETAIL & SPECIAL SALES	Tom Mifsud
DIRECTOR OF FINANCE	Tricia Griffin
ASSISTANT MARKETING DIRECTOR	Ann Marie Doherty
PREPRESS MANAGER	Emily Rabin
BOOK PRODUCTION MANAGER	Jonathan Polsky

SPECIAL THANKS TO:

Bozena Bannett; Alexandra Bliss; Mary Cadley; Bernadette Corbie; Robert Dente; Gina Di Meglio;
Anne-Michelle Gallero; Peter Harper; Suzanne Janso; Robert Marasco; Natalie McCrea; Margarita Quiogue;
Mary Jane Rigoroso; Steven Sandonato; Mark A. Schmidt; Grace Sullivan; Cornelis Verwaal

*

COVER PICTURE CREDITS:

Hardcover edition front cover: Hodalic—Saola—Gamma.
Back cover, clockwise from top: José Fuste Raga—Corbis;
Scala—Art Resource, NY; Courtesy Santiago Calatrava S.A.;
Premium Stock—Corbis; Tom Bonner—L.A. Philharmonic; Christopher Little—Corbis

Softcover edition front cover, center: Hodalic—Saola—Gamma.
Insets, from top: Tom Bonner—L.A. Philharmonic; Scala—Art Resource, NY;
Christopher Little—Corbis; Courtesy Santiago Calatrava S.A.; Premium Stock—Corbis
Back cover: José Fuste Raga—Corbis

Copyright 2004 Time Inc. Home Entertainment
Published by TIME Books
Time Inc. • 1271 Avenue of the Americas • New York, NY 10020

All rights reserved. No part of this book may be reproduced in any form or by any electronic or mechanical means,
including information storage and retrieval systems, without permission in writing from the publisher, except by a reviewer,
who may quote brief passages in a review. TIME and the Red Border Design are protected through trademark registration
in the United States and in the foreign countries where TIME magazine circulates.

First Edition
ISBN: 1-932273-23-9
Library of Congress Control Number: 2004104204

TIME is a trademark of Time Inc.

We welcome your comments and suggestions about TIME Books. Please write to us at
TIME Books • Attention: Book Editors • PO Box 11016 • Des Moines, IA 50336-1016

If you would like to order any of our hardcover Collector's Edition books, please call us at 1-800-327-6388.
(Monday through Friday, 7 a.m.–8 p.m., or Saturday, 7 a.m.–6 p.m., Central time)

PRINTED IN THE UNITED STATES OF AMERICA

TIME

Great Buildings Of the World

HANS WOLF—GETTY IMAGES

The World's Most Influential, Inspiring And Astonishing Structures

SPRINGDALE PUBLIC LIBRARY
405 S. PLEASANT ST.
SPRINGDALE, AR 72764

CONTENTS

GUGGENHEIM MUSEUM, BILBAO, SPAIN, 1997
Architect Frank Gehry

JOSE FUSTE RAGA—CORBIS

CHRYSLER BUILDING, NEW YORK CITY, 1930
Architect: William van Alen

Seven Ways of Looking at a Building

BURSTING OUT OF THE LONG SHAFT OF NEW YORK CITY'S Chrysler Building, the seven soaring arches that form its spire appear to have materialized from a Buck Rogers comic strip. This is a building that demands attention: "Look at me!" And look we do, admiring the way architect William Van Alen somehow managed to snare the idea of ascent and express it in steel. You don't have to be a historian to sense that this urgent shape reflects all the giddy gaiety of the late 1920s, still crazy after all these years.

Engineers admire the spire for its cladding of Nirosta steel, a new alloy at the time, which makes it shimmer in the light of a full moon. Academics read it as an example of the streamlined Art Deco style. Lovers of biography savor it as the product of a stormy collaboration between the bull-headed auto baron who commissioned it and the Paris-educated dreamer who designed it. And everyone can love the spire because it's beautiful, and a thing of beauty is a joy forever.

In recent decades, some of the joy seemed to vanish from architecture. Most buildings that hankered after greatness sought to find it in serenity and clarity—admirable qualities but not exciting ones. Then, in 1997, the Guggenheim Museum opened a new building in Bilbao, Spain, designed by Frank Gehry, a Toronto-born Californian whose work was admired by design buffs but little known to the general public.

Bilbao put an end to Gehry the cult figure. People loved the building, loved its swooping, shimmering forms, so slippery you couldn't seem to get your mind around them. Gehry's structure looked as if he had detonated a bomb in one of Ludwig Mies van der Rohe's pared-down modernist buildings, frozen the explosion two seconds later, then dipped the result in titanium. Who knew buildings could be this much fun? Or this strange and challenging? Who dared to think that a contemporary building could be awe inspiring?

Frank Gehry did. And with a single building, he made architecture exciting again. We offer no polls to prove this contention, no scientific studies to support it. But in the years since 1997, people have been buzzing about buildings: Norman Foster's transparent dome for the Reichstag in Berlin; Santiago Calatrava's wing-flapping Milwaukee Art Museum; Daniel Libeskind's haunting Jewish Museum of Berlin.

So the moment seems right for TIME to explore the subject of the world's most fascinating buildings. In selecting them, we've been guided by the many meanings one can read into the spire of the Chrysler Building, for different buildings are great in different ways. In a 1917 poem, Wallace Stevens invited readers to consider "Thirteen Ways of Looking at a Blackbird." Following his lead, we've collected our criteria into Seven Ways of Looking at a Building, the seven prisms through which we chose the buildings we've featured.

As *witness to history.* Some buildings are significant because of the stories they tell, the information they contain. The House of the Vettii in Pompeii was not an outstanding structure in its time, but the window it offers us on life in the Roman Empire is irreplaceable. Modern-day buildings can be just as revelatory: when renovating Germany's Reichstag, Foster retained graffiti scrawled on the walls by conquering Russian soldiers in 1945.

As *object of beauty.* As the museum in Bilbao reminds us, a building can be memorable simply because it is exhilarating to behold. Centuries after the Taj Mahal was built, it is visited by tens of thousands of people each year for the simple reason that it thrills our eyes and exalts our spirit.

As *exemplar of style.* This book is not a history of design, but we have selected certain buildings because they encapsulate an era in style, from the sinuous motifs of Victor Horta's Art Nouveau home in Brussels to the Pop Art playfulness of Richard Rogers' and Renzo Piano's Pompidou Centre in Paris.

As *artifact of technology.* Certain buildings are beacons: the Pantheon in Rome is the space that launched a thousand domes, and the great iron-and-glass grid of London's Crystal Palace demonstrated that Industrial Age materials could create an entirely new kind of structure. The weird shapes of Gehry's Bilbao museum were made possible by computer software originally created for aircraft designers.

As *emblem of a culture.* In the great swoop of Eero Saarinen's TWA Terminal in New York City, we sense America's love of speed; in the extravagances of the Paris Opera House, we find a society entranced by display. Likewise, the Taj Mahal and Alhambra are not only beautiful; they are also stone books in which we can read the varying aspirations of Islamic culture as expressed in medieval Spain and Mogul India.

As *the work of an architect.* Every building is to some extent a work of art. And since it is fascinating to trace the stylistic evolution of artists, this book offers portfolios featuring the work of five noted architects, including Calatrava, whose buildings are often inspired by his paintings and sculptures.

As *repository of social values.* The home of the Dalai Lama in Tibet, the Potala Palace, consists of two distinct buildings: the Red Palace, devoted to religion, bestrides the White Palace, devoted to government. The social heirarchy is set in stone. Buildings express our deepest values: when the home of Britain's Parliament burned down in 1836, M.P.s mandated that the new building must be built in Gothic Revival style: certainly it was not fit for them to meet under the domes and pediments of the "pagan," neoclassical style.

Are there more ways of looking at a building? Of course. To discover them, turn the page and open your eyes.

—*Kelly Knauer*

GRANT FAINT-GETTY IMAGES

TAJ MAHAL, AKRA, INDIA
Rudyard Kipling called this elegant 17th century mausoleum "a sigh made of stone"

Buildings that Astonish

Architects like to talk in terms of form and function. But some of our favorite buildings were simply built to thrill—and utility be damned. Yes, the Sydney Opera House is a home for great music, but it could have taken the form of a simple box, rather than evoking a stunning array of billowing sails. And what good is the Taj Mahal if not simply to inspire? In this chapter, we present buildings whose architects dared to ask, "What if …?"

MASSIMO BORCHI—ATLANTIDE

Travelers from An Antique Land

The **Great Pyramids at Giza** are messengers from the past that present more questions than answers

VERBATIM
"Soldiers! Forty centuries behold you!"—Napoleon to his troops, on the eve of the 1798 battle that won control of Egypt for France

WHILE WE DON'T KNOW IF HE SENT POSTCARDS home, we do know that Herodotus, the ancient Greek historian, visited Egypt in 450 B.C. and observed that "in his desire to excel all who ruled Egypt before him, this king left a pyramid of brick to commemorate his name." The king in question was Khufu (Cheops, to the Greeks), who ruled over the land of Kemet ("Black," a reference to the rich, life-giving soil deposited by the flooding Nile each spring) in the 25th century B.C. It is a measure of the near unfathomable age of this last survivor from the original Seven Wonders of the World that when Herodotus wrote these words, he was chronologically closer to Columbus' discovery of the New World than he was to Khufu's time. Although earlier Egyptian kings had built pyramids as tombs, Khufu was able to exploit Egypt's growing size, prosperity and technical ability to create a monument that would dwarf all that came before it. His Great Pyramid at Giza, the tallest of three, was originally 481 ft. high, but time, the elements and human mischief have whittled it down to 449 ft. It still ranks among the most massive—and the most mysterious—of mankind's creations.

The pyramids breed conjecture. Herodotus, whose civilization relied on slavery, believed they had been erected by forced labor. (It now appears that young men from around the kingdom would voluntarily journey to Giza during the Nile's flood season to join in the work, a service that brought great honor.) Napoleon thought they were the granaries used by Joseph in the Old Testament to save Egypt from famine. (They weren't.) In the centuries between, nearly every regal visitor, from Alexander the Great to Julius Caesar, was hypnotized by the pyramids' majesty and humbled by their mysteries.

Among the puzzles: how people who had not invented the wheel and had no sophisticated mechanical devices for hoisting large, heavy objects off the ground were able to haul more than 2 million giant stone blocks (weighing as much as nine tons each) from quarries many miles distant and then raise them hundreds of feet in the air. For that matter, how did the ancient Egyptians design a building in which the relationship of the overall height to the length of each side is the same as the ratio of a circle's radius to its circumference, thousands of years before the Greeks discovered π? We don't even know with certainty what the people of Kemet called their timeless structures; *pyramid* is derived from the Greek.

During the 45 centuries that these questions have haunted human imagination, we have learned a little and destroyed a lot. Graverobbers looted the royal tombs within the three pyramids at Giza long before Herodotus arrived. The smooth white limestone cladding that once brilliantly reflected the desert sunlight in all directions was scavenged in the 7th century by Muslim builders, to adorn their own cities. And Napoleon's troops amused themselves in idle hours by shooting the nose off the Sphinx. Today, pollution from nearby Cairo threatens the pyramids, as does nonstop tourist traffic. Still they stand, so immovable as to seem immortal. As an Egyptian adage goes, man fears time, and time fears the pyramids. ∎

DAVID SUTHERLAND—STONE—GETTY IMAGES

HILARIE KAVANAGH—STONE—GETTY IMAGES

ASTONISH

A Shah's Vision of Paradise

It was crafted by 20,000 workers over a period of 22 years—and it shows.
India's ethereal **Taj Mahal** may be the world's single most famous building

MARK TWAIN CALLED IT "THAT SOARING BUBBLE OF marble." For Rudyard Kipling, it was "the Ivory Gate through which all good dreams come." For the great Indian poet, Rabindranath Tagore, it was "a teardrop of love on the cheek of time." But for Shah Jahan, the 17th century Mogul Emperor who built the Taj Mahal ("Crown Palace") in Agra, the building was a tribute to the woman he loved. After the death in 1631 of his favorite wife, Mumtaz Mahal ("Exalted One of the Palace"), with whom he had 14 children in 19 years, the Shah resolved to build an

earthly representation of paradise. From the farthest reaches of his empire (which included parts of present-day India, Afghanistan, Pakistan and Bangladesh), he summoned architects, stonemasons and artisans—some 20,000 of them—who labored for more than two decades on the royal mausoleum.

Because Islamic belief forbids graphic representations of the divine, this vision of eternity is evoked, not stated; it is a tale told in geometry and proportion, symmetry and balance. Clad entirely in white marble, the Taj Mahal rises more than 200 ft. over a garden with four canals representing the Four

MANSELL COLLECTION—TIME LIFE PICTURES

LEGEND
Shah Jahan ordered his chief stonemason's hand cut off, so that he could never create a rival to the Taj Mahal

UNITED Shah Jahan ("Ruler of the Universe") and wife Mumtaz Mahal were unusually close for an Islamic royal couple of the 17th century: she accompanied him on military campaigns and advised him on matters of state. Jahan, who was deposed by his son, never built a planned—and equally splendid— tomb for himself that was to occupy a site across the Yamuna River from the Taj Mahal, so he was interred alongside his wife. Since her crypt occupies the precise midpoint of the building, however, his was placed slightly off-center (below), violating the careful symmetry that his builders labored so hard to achieve

ROLAND & SABRINA MICHAUD— WOODFIN CAMP

Rivers of Paradise, which are said to flow with water, milk, wine and honey. The walls of the building are inlaid with black stone calligraphy, citing verses from the Koran on the rewards due to the just in the next life. The elegant white dome resembles a giant pearl floating above the building's four minarets, recalling the Prophet Muhammad's vision of the throne of God as a pearl surrounded by four pillars. It is on just such a throne that Shah Jahan believed God would sit in judgment of him, before welcoming him into paradise—and the arms of the wife he had lost. ∎

If This Be Madness . . .

Built by a Romantic whose disposition was antic, **Schloss Neuschwanstein** helped end the reign of Bavaria's King Ludwig II—but we still think it rules

ONCE UPON A TIME THERE LIVED IN BAVARIA A YOUNG prince who read too many fairy tales and had too much money—a circumstance guaranteed to alarm royal ministers and excite royal architects. The time was the 1860s, the raging height of the Romantic movement, when the sorrows of Young Werther and the operas of Richard Wagner stirred German souls. The prince was Ludwig, of the house of Wittelsbach, who became King Ludwig II of Bavaria at only 18, in 1864. And the result of his obsessions was a series of madly romantic, madly lavish, madly expensive castles, the most famed of which is Schloss Neuschwanstein, near Oberammergau. Did we mention that this royal builder is known to history as "Mad" King Ludwig?

Sadly, King Ludwig II did not live happily ever after. His ministers, fed up with his extravagances, had him declared insane in 1886, when he was only 40, and placed him under *schloss* arrest on one of his more mundane estates. A doctor was assigned to care for him; three days later both doctor and patient drowned in a nearby lake. The deaths were never explained. More than a century later, Ludwig's over-the-top buildings cast the kind of spell that even ministers understand; they are major attractions for Bavarian tourism.

If Neuschwanstein looks familiar—that's because it's the template for Walt Disney's knock-offs at Disneyland and Disney World. Like the Disney versions, its inside is incomplete: Ludwig's ministers pulled the plug after 17 years of construction, before the castle was finished. Then again, Neuschwanstein, like Disneyland, was never intended to be much more than a stimulating stage set. It's pure Bavarian hokum—Schlock Neuschwanstein—but a man can dream, can't he? ∎

PREMIUM STOCK—CORBIS

ADAM WOOLFITT—CORBIS (2)

80 ROOMS, GREAT VIEWS: Ludwig was dethroned before the interior of Schloss Neuschwanstein (the Swan's Stone) could be finished, but some rooms came near completion. At left is the three-story Throne Room, adorned in Byzantine style, complete with inlaid camels on the floor. The ivory-and-gold throne Ludwig commissioned for the room was not completed. Above, a detail of a swan atop the royal washstand displays intricate carved craftsmanship; Ludwig's lavish ways kept an army of builders, artists and craftsmen employed at royal expense. The couple in the mural are Wagner's medieval lovers, Tristan and Isolde. The castle also includes a lavish Singers' Hall, inspired by Wagner's *Der Meistersinger;* Ludwig befriended the composer as a young man

VERBATIM
"Unique one! Holy one! How glorious!
So full of rapture! To drown ... unconscious"
—Ludwig, letter to Wagner

A Whole New Slant on Art

You could put a passel of Picassos in New York City's **Guggenheim Museum,** and there would still be only one star of the show: Frank Lloyd Wright

ARVIND GARG—STONE—GETTY IMAGES

WHEN COPPER MAGNATE SOLOMON GUGGENHEIM decided to build a lavish, namesake palace to show off his impressive collection of modern art, he turned to Frank Lloyd Wright. It was an odd choice: Wright famously hated cities, and he hated New York City with special bile. The crusty architect immediately began lobbying to have the museum moved away from Guggenheim's site—a choice block on Manhattan's Fifth Avenue, facing Central Park—and into the park itself, where the natural environment would better suit his "organic" style. Losing that argument, Wright resolved to rebel pointedly against the city's right-angled, linear grid (and the architectural establishment that resided within it) by designing a circular building.

For what would be his last major work, Wright dreamed up an "optimistic ziggurat"—a sloping white spiral that would guide visitors along a quarter-mile-long ramp, along which artworks would hang on walls that leaned outward at the same angle as an artist's easel. A glass dome at the spiral's summit would bathe the exhibits in natural light. The design, which Wright tweaked for 17 years, was so unusual that a construction firm specializing in parking garages and freeway ramps was retained to build it.

When artists learned what Wright had wrought, they rebelled. Willem de Kooning, Robert Motherwell and Franz Kline signed an open letter to the museum's directors, protesting that Wright's "curvilinear slope indicates a callous disregard for the fundamental rectilinear frame of reference." Wright retorted that no such frame existed, except when cultivated "by callous disregard of nature, all too common in your art." Wright was wrong, and the artists were right: the museum's walls curve; paintings don't. And the narrow width of Wright's sloping ramp forces the viewer to stand closer to the paintings than many would like. But for Wright, these cavils were beside the point. He was trying to bring visitors into a more intimate relationship with art than most museums offered and also to make them look beyond the collection to the world around them—or, at least, the design around them. ∎

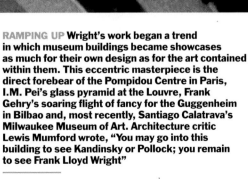

J. ALEX LANGLEY

RAMPING UP Wright's work began a trend in which museum buildings became showcases as much for their own design as for the art contained within them. This eccentric masterpiece is the direct forebear of the Pompidou Centre in Paris, I.M. Pei's glass pyramid at the Louvre, Frank Gehry's soaring flight of fancy for the Guggenheim in Bilbao and, most recently, Santiago Calatrava's Milwaukee Museum of Art. Architecture critic Lewis Mumford wrote, "You may go into this building to see Kandinsky or Pollock; you remain to see Frank Lloyd Wright"

Aria for an Orange Peel

Millions of hearts have lifted at the sight of the wonder Down Under, the **Sydney Opera House,** but guess who hasn't seen it? Architect Joern Utzon

WHAT THE EIFFEL TOWER IS TO PARIS, THE OPERA House is to Sydney, Australia: beloved icon, skyline tattoo, fallback photo-op. In its trademark interlocking white shells, observers have seen a giant armadillo, oysters and the pointed helmets of Spanish conquistadors. But architect Joern Utzon says his design was inspired by the simple act of peeling an orange: the 14 shells of the building, if combined, would form a perfect sphere.

In 1957, Utzon was virtually unknown outside his native Denmark when his entry in the design contest for the new Opera House was singled out by one of the judges, Eero Saarinen, who called it a work of genius and declared he could not endorse any other choice. (In contrast, Ludwig Mies van der Rohe turned his back when introduced to Utzon, then 39.)

Utzon's complex structure confounded the engineers who built it. They estimated the project would cost $10 million and require three years' building time; they were only off by $40 million and 13 years. Long before the structure was finished, Utzon was—he was officially given the sack in 1966. When his masterpiece was officially opened by Queen Elizabeth II in 1973, the architect was not invited to the ceremony, nor was his name mentioned. To this day, he has never returned to Australia and thus has never set eyes upon his creation, easily one of the most beloved buildings on the planet.

For in the years since 1973, something unexpected happened. Sydneysiders—and the world—fell in love with Utzon's vision. Perched dramatically on a peninsula thrusting into Sydney Harbor, its lofty shells are covered by 1 million creamy white tiles that reflect the colors of sunlight and water throughout the city. At least one woman who had planned to commit suicide by jumping from the nearby Sydney Harbor Bridge was moved to reconsider because of the beauty of Utzon's design. And slowly, the rift between the Opera House board and Utzon has begun to heal. In 1995, Utzon, then 77, was lionized as the hero of Alan John's opera, *The Eighth Wonder,* based on the creation of the Aussies' cherished landmark. The world premiere of the work was staged at the Sydney Opera House, and we're betting a fat lady sang. ∎

DALE BOYER—STONE—GETTY IMAGES

VERBATIM
The Sydney Opera House is "a marvelous and inseparable part of my life."
—Joern Utzon, 2004

Architecture's New Wave

Less is more? No, more is more at Santiago Calatrava's **Tenerife Opera House,** whose cresting concrete tsunami has but one function: to delight

SWEEPING OVER THE TOP OF SPANISH ARCHITECT SANTIAGO CALATRAVA'S spectacular new Opera House in Tenerife in the Canary Islands, a gigantic concrete wave shelters the cone-shaped auditorium complex. But this wave is more than a wave: it's a thumb in the eye of the modernist style that dominated 20th century architecture. Led by the German-born giants Walter Gropius and Ludwig Mies van der Rohe, and marching under their banners—less is more; form follows function—modernists took an Occam's razor to the highly embellished designs of the 19th century. Stripping decoration and ornament from buildings, they produced structures of serene purity and rigor. But as the style penetrated the mainstream, the rich materials and symmetries that distinguished the masters' work went missing—and the result was a generation of banal, boxy buildings that argued rather persuasively that "less is less."

But there were other significant strains of 20th century architecture, which delighted in the play of forms upon one another and in the ability of new materials to create shapes never seen before. Architects working in this vein often looked back to the work of Antonio Gaudí, a Spaniard, whose works, like the unfinished cathedral La Sagrada Familia, displayed an exuberant delight in fluidly organic shapes that made Modernism seem fussy and prim. The influence of Gaudí can be seen in Joern Utzon's Sydney Opera House and Eero Saarinen's TWA Terminal in New York City. And now, in the first years of a new century, the heirs of Gaudí seem to be in the ascendant: the overwhelming public embrace of American architect Frank Gehry's swooping, flowing Guggenheim Museum in Bilbao, Spain, showed that people were hungry for new shapes. Calatrava, a Spanish architect whose works often are inspired by natural forms, is poised to become architecture's next superstar. As for what function his wave fills, he answers, defiantly: None. ∎

ALAN KARCHMER—ESTO (2)

SWOOSH! The $80 million Opera House opened in September 2003 in Santa Cruz, Tenerife's main city (yes, with more landscaping than the work-in-progress picture at left shows). The cone-shaped auditorium complex holds two concert halls, the larger of which, above, seats 1,668 people. The architect, who often finds inspiration in his own sculptures and drawings, as well as from the natural world, says the building's shape was suggested by Mount Teide, the volcano overlooking Tenerife, into whose dormant cone tourists can descend. Unlike Eero Saarinen, who dismissed suggestions that his swooping TWA Terminal in New York City was based on a bird in flight, Calatrava happily admits that the 200-ft.-high, 3,500-ton concrete canopy atop the building suggests a wave … and a shell … and a seabird's wing. The outer skin of the building is covered with broken ceramic tiles that gleam in sunlight or moonlight

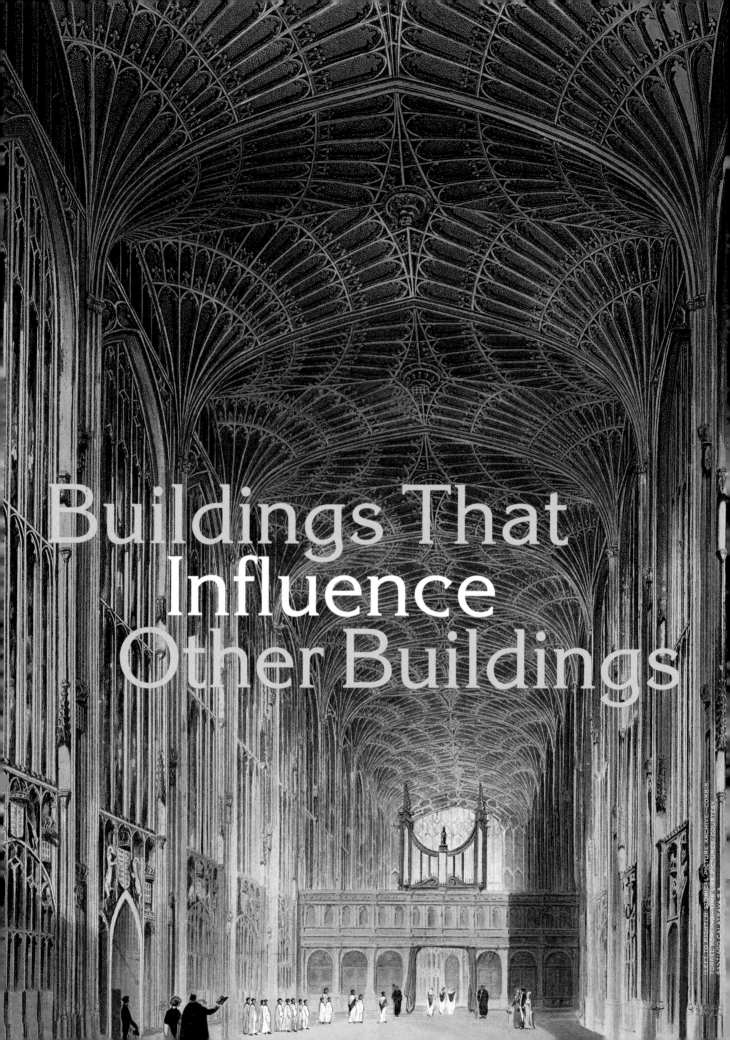

Buildings That Influence Other Buildings

LEFT TO RIGHT: HISTORICAL PICTURE ARCHIVE—CORBIS;
TORKEL MORNING TIME LIFE PICTURES; COURTESY
SANTIAGO CALATRAVA S.A.

A roof is a roof is a roof, whether it's inspiring worshippers in the 16th century King's College Chapel in Cambridge, U.K., keeping 1930s roadsters dry in a Frank Lloyd Wright parking garage in Wisconsin or sheltering commuters at a Lisbon train station designed by Santiago Calatrava. But if function in design is static, form is ever changing. As the fan-vaulting style that turns a ceiling into an upside-down lily pond is interpreted through the ages, it evolves in delightful ways: new materials like reinforced concrete and plate glass interact with the unique aesthetic of an individual architect to create a set of wonderful variations on a theme. "Eternity is in love with the productions of time," said William Blake. And so are we

THEME AND VARIATIONS
King's College Chapel, 1515
Johnson Wax Building, 1939
Oriente Train Station, 1998

The Man-Made Mountain

Pyramid's progress: from Egypt to Mexico, San Francisco to Las Vegas

The Pyramids at Giza

TransAmerica Building

T IS NO COINCIDENCE THAT PYRAMIDS ARE AMONG THE first buildings erected by many civilizations, often following soon after the development of earthen mounds, structures that are not quite buildings themselves but nonetheless give tangible form to man's desire to shape his immediate environment. As early cultures acquired the ability to bake mud or clay into bricks, and later to cut rock into building stones, pyramids became the natural next step in the development of the large man-made structure.

Mounds and pyramids mimic nature, duplicating the form of the mountains and hills believed by many early cultures to be sacred. To create an artificial mountain was to channel into human hands the power of the gods. Hence ancient pyramids were often seen as gateways between this world and the next. Early builders were attracted to the form for a less exalted reason: the pyramid requires only rudimentary engineering skill—and its shape ensures it won't fall down, the self-evident reason why so many of them have lasted thousands of years.

The pyramid's appeal is timeless. Fashion-obsessed Romans began adorning their homes and jewelry with the pointed shape after they conquered Egypt in 30 B.C. The Maya, the Masons and Mozart found mystical magic in the form: crowned with an eye, it appears on the dollar bill in your pocket. New Age thinkers say its shape channels energy to those beneath it, but we think the flow is the other way around: rooted in this world but pointing toward heaven, the pyramid is the alpha form of the architecture of aspiration. ■

STEPHEN STUDD—GETTY IMAGES

TRAVEL LIBRARY—ROBERT HARDING

Luxor Hotel

New York Life Building

PYRAMIDS AT GIZA Egypt's first Pharaohs were buried in earthen mounds called mastabas. Eventually, these mounds were fashioned from mud bricks placed one on top of another, each brick slightly smaller than the one below it. These were the world's first step pyramids. Later still, when cut stone replaced mud bricks, the load-bearing capacity of the pyramid increased exponentially, making it possible to build taller pyramids with smooth walls

LUXOR HOTEL AND CASINO, 1993 At 30 stories, the Las Vegas Luxor pyramid is not quite as big as the originals at Giza, but its $375 million price tag probably dwarfs that of the genuine article. That budget bought architect Veldon Simpson 2,526 rooms, a 100,000-sq.-ft. casino, a Sphinx with laser-beam eyes and a spotlight on top of the pyramid that projects a 40 billion-candlepower beam into the sky—for reasons that remain obscure but may involve publicity

TRANSAMERICA BUILDING, 1972 Architect William Pereira described his design for the 853-ft. tower as "classical," but critics called what was then the tallest man-made structure west of Chicago a "dunce cap." Three decades later, the TransAmerica pyramid has joined cable cars and the Golden Gate Bridge (whose towers it tops) as an icon of the city. Its base is fortified with 16,000 cu. yds. of concrete and reinforced with 300 miles of steel rods

NEW YORK LIFE BUILDING, MANHATTAN, 1928 For the peak of his 40-story Gothic Revival New York Life Insurance Co. building, architect Cass Gilbert sculpted the pyramid form into an octagonal, 88-ft.-tall pinnacle, sheathed in gold leaf and copper. The building's top, which culminates in a lantern, shimmers at dawn and twilight, much as the original pyramids at Giza reflected sunlight before their white limestone coating was stripped away

TOP: B.S.P.I.—CORBIS; BOTTOM: GAIL MOONEY—CORBIS

"Il Duomo"

THIS PAGE: PHOTOS12.COM-POLARIS. OPPOSITE CLOCKWISE FROM TOP: PAUL CHESLEY—GETTY IMAGES; MICHAEL ROUGIER—TIME LIFE PICTURES; ADAM WOOLFITT—CORBIS

INFLUENCE

A Thinking Cap for Buildings

As old as Rome and as modern as the millennium, the dome is an eternal form

AMONG THE FUNDAMENTAL BUILDING BLOCKS OF architecture—the cube, pyramid, arch and so on—one shape is unique. The dome has no straight lines, edges, angles or flat surfaces. But this form is also supremely functional: the geometry of domes is such that they enclose the greatest space within the least surface area of any possible design. Once reserved for houses of God, domes have inspired architects and congregations for 2,000 years, crowning temples, churches, synagogues and mosques throughout Europe, the Middle East and Asia.

One of the first builders to realize the power of the dome was the Roman general Agrippa, whose Pantheon was a magnificent temple dedicated to all of Rome's gods. Rebuilt by the Emperor Hadrian in A.D. 118, the Pantheon is topped by an oculus, or "eye," which projects a dramatic shaft of sunlight onto the floor, sweeping across the interior like a slowly moving spotlight throughout the day. For 13 centuries, the Pantheon was the world's largest dome. But when Rome fell, the dome went into decline: the engineering behind the big hemispheres was lost to Western Europe for hundreds of years. By the Middle Ages, architect-engineers were far more interested in the buttressed arches that took their buildings high into the sky than in forms inherited from antiquity.

Renaissance genius Filippo Brunelleschi, who spent much of his life working on the dome of Florence's Cathedral of Santa Maria del Fiore, restored the dome to prominence. "ll Duomo" sparked a revival of the form, influencing Andrea Palladio, Christopher Wren and Thomas Jefferson. Five centuries later, a renaissance man of a different sort, polymath inventor R. Buckminster Fuller, took the ancient shape into a new era with his geodesic dome, an elegant honeycomb of tetrahedrons (pyramids with three upright sides) forming a hemisphere. Inexpensive, easy to erect and so lightweight they often don't need a foundation, geodesic domes offer the greatest strength-to-weight ratio of any architectural form.

In 2000 Richard Rogers' 160-ft.-high Millennium Dome opened in London, sheltering 20 acres of space under its vast roof, which is partially suspended from large pylons. The exposition inside was universally pronounced a bust, but the dome had made a triumphal entry into a new century. ■

20

THE PANTHEON, ROME, A.D. 118: Caesar Augustus' general, Agrippa, built this magnificent temple over a filled-in swamp; when the building subsided and cracked, it was demolished and rebuilt by the Emperor Hadrian in A.D. 118. Its mighty dome has a diameter of 142 ft. and stands 142 ft. high, forming a perfect half-sphere. The oculus at top is thus suspended at the precise vertical point at which the dome would rest if the (imaginary) complete sphere were touching the ground

Church of Our Savior

U.S. Pavilion

"IL DUOMO," FLORENCE, 1434
The ribbed skeleton directs the dome's weight down, not out, allowing it to be built with interior supports and no outer scaffolding. It is hollow, consisting of an inner and outer shell, reducing its mass

CHURCH OF OUR SAVIOR ON THE SPILLED BLOOD, ST. PETERSBURG, 1907 Russian architects took Islam's pointed dome and twisted it it into an onion shape, as in this church built on the spot where Czar Alexander II was assassinated in 1881

U.S. PAVILION, EXPO 67, MONTREAL, 1967 Made of an aluminum grid and glass or plastic inserts, geodesic domes are lightweight but strong. Buckminster Fuller's dome for Expo 67 stood 200 ft. tall and had a diameter of 250 ft.

The Pillar and the Pediment

History's most influential design style is dormant, pending another Palladio

WHEN RENAISSANCE ARCHITECT ANDREA PALLADIO began updating the classical styles of ancient Greece and Rome in the early 16th century, he created history's single most influential design vernacular. For the next half-millennium, designers of structures that sought to embody prestige, dignity and legitimacy—from Thomas Jefferson to Adolf Hitler's favorite architect, Albert Speer—followed Palladio's lead into a garden of Euclidean delights, and thousands of pillared and pedimented porticoes bloomed.

Emphasizing mathematical symmetry, the neoclassical style and its stately geometries were perfectly suited to the Age of Reason—Jefferson's era—which explains why a stroll through America's capital city can resemble a field trip to Rome. The Jefferson Memorial echoes the dome of the Pantheon, as well as Palladio's Villa Rotonda; the Lincoln Memorial evokes the Parthenon in Athens. Yet neoclassical monumentality can contend with the ideals it seeks to declare. Cass Gilbert's U.S. Supreme Court building argues persuasively for the importance of the goings-on inside it but comes off as a forbidding, autocratic edifice. In contrast, Norman Foster's transparent dome for the renovated Re- ichstag in Berlin *(see page 42)* demonstrates that public buildings can be both imposing and openly inclusive.

Modernists like Ludwig Mies van der Rohe dismissed neoclassicism as a tired architectural lie, and their sleek, unadorned masterpieces drove a stake through its heart for decades. But Philip Johnson, long a leading advocate of the International Style, broke with Miesian minimalism in 1984 with his radical design for the AT&T Building in Manhattan. A self-conscious attempt to create a postmodern aesthetic, his building boasted a discernible base with a towering, 110-ft. arched entryway and a definite midsection whose windows evoked columns. It was topped off with a broken pediment whose form defiantly served no earthly function, aside from reminding observers of a Chippendale highboy.

But Johnson's gambit, while stimulating and essential at the time, did not lead to a stirring revival of the classical vernacular. For now, with architects like Foster, Frank Gehry and Santiago Calatrava inventing radical new forms that have no use for pillars and pediments, the classical style is lifeless: consigned to the showy entryways stuck onto suburban McMansions, Palladio's tributes to Greece and Rome are now hollow emblems of grandiosity. ■

JAMES P BLAIR—CORBIS

Jefferson Memorial

Jefferson Memorial

AT&T Building

ALAN SCHEIN PHOTOGRAPHY—CORBIS (2)

JEFFERSON MEMORIAL, 1943
Architect John Russell Pope adapted the Roman dome that Jefferson had employed in his designs for his home, Monticello, and the Rotunda of the University of Virginia; Pope added a portico and colonnade

AT&T BUILDING, NEW YORK CITY, 1984 Philip Johnson's historical allusions sounded the death knell for stripped-down modernism, but his classical elements are simply grafted onto a modern building and did not point the way to a valid new style

LINCOLN MEMORIAL, 1922
Henry Bacon based the monument on the Parthenon in Athens, minus a triangular pediment. The 36 Doric columns represent the states that made up the newly preserved Union at the time of Lincoln's death

U.S. SUPREME COURT, 1939
Cass Gilbert, who once called this design "the most important and notable work of my life," had to lobby dictator Benito Mussolini to obtain the finest marble from Italy's best quarries for the courtroom within

Lincoln Memorial

U.S. Supreme Court

LEFT: PETER GRIDLEY—GETTY IMAGES; RIGHT: OWEN FRANKEN—CORBIS

Buildings for "Barbarians"

A brilliant synthesis of height and light, the Gothic style keeps coming back

THE TERM GOTHIC WAS UNKNOWN TO THE ARCHITECTS OF the Middle Ages who practiced the style. They called their idiom—marked by soaring walls with vast windows—the "French style," for the country from which it sprang, through the midwifery of a Benedictine Abbot named Suger in the year 1144. That was when Suger unveiled the rebuilt abbey and church of St. Denis, outside Paris.

Designed by an architect whose name is lost to history, St. Denis combines the pointed arch with the ribbed vault to support vast amounts of weight, thus relieving walls of their traditional burden of holding up the roof—in a seemingly miraculous new way. In tandem, these innovations meant that the church walls could be thinner and punctured by many large windows that would allow sunlight, tinted by stained glass, to stream inside as never before. This marvel both inspired worshippers and attracted travelers, thus en-

riching Suger's abbey. Within a century, bishoprics throughout Europe wanted to emulate St. Denis' success (and cash flow) by erecting French-style cathedrals of their own. The Cathedral at Chartres added the use of flying buttresses, allowing the building to soar 120 ft. into the air. In Britain, the spire of Salisbury Cathedral stretches 404 ft. into the sky.

By the 1500s, the French style had nearly run its course; the term Gothic was coined by Renaissance architects as an insult that equated the idiom's excessive ornamentation to the supposed vulgarity of the Barbarian Goth tribes of northern Europe. Neoclassicism had a long run in the centuries after the Renaissance, but in the 1900s Gothic Revival emerged as a counterweight to Greek and Roman forms. As recently as 1984, Philip Johnson was adapting modernism's signature glass curtain wall to Gothic forms. Soaring with uplift, the "French style" may yet be around for a while. ∎

PPG Building

Chateau Frontenac

CHATEAU FRONTENAC, QUEBEC CITY, 1924 Architect Bruce Price's design is the finest example of Canadian "Chateau style," which melds Gothic design elements with Tudor accents and northern European ski chalet motifs. The form is found in many of the Canadian Pacific Railway's large hotels

PPG BUILDING, PITTSBURGH, PA., 1984 Architect Philip Johnson said that this design is "the only building I've done that Prince Charles likes" (the heir to Britain's throne favors traditional styles). The five-acre, 40-story PPG complex also refers to nearby landmarks: the Allegheny County Courthouse and the University of Pittsburgh's 42-story skyscraper, the Cathedral of Learning

TRIBUNE TOWER, CHICAGO, 1925 In 1922, Raymond Hood and John M. Howells won a competition to design a skyscraper to house the city's major newspaper. Their winning design, topped with eight flying buttresses, was modeled on France's Rouen Cathedral and Belgium's Cathedral of St. Rombaut

Tribune Tower

SALISBURY CATHEDRAL, 1266: Most Gothic cathedrals took a century or more to build, but this great church was erected in a single generation, which gives it an unusual cohesion of design. Its 404-ft. spire is still the tallest in Britain

PPG BUILDING: W. CODY-CORBIS; CHATEAU FRONTENAC: ANN ARTHUS-BERTRAND-CORBIS; TRIBUNE TOWER: UNDER WOOD & UNDERWOOD-CORBIS; SALISBURY CATHEDRAL & CHOIR: NIK WHEELER

Where Power Resides

PIAZZA DEL CAMPIDOGLIO, ROME
Michelangelo revitalized two older buildings
by adding a third and creating a new plaza
with a commanding view of Rome

The architecture of power reflects our changing view of authority. Consider the first and last entries in this chapter: centuries ago, the Maya walked up the steps of a pyramid to be killed by priests as an offering to the gods. Today, residents of Berlin ascend the spiral ramp of the Reichstag's great glass dome to look down on the chamber below, where representatives shape the laws that govern them. From stone pyramid to glass dome, architecture charts the journey from priestly tyranny to democratic transparency

RICHARD T. NOWITZ—CORBIS

Sacred Site of Sacrifice

It is a triumph of engineering and astronomy, but the **Pyramid of the Sorcerer** was also the scene of bloody ritual killings

A T THE CENTER OF UXMAL, THE MOST EXOTIC OF THE ancient cities in the Yucatán region of Mexico, the Pyramid of the Sorcerer rises into the sky. Unique among Maya pyramids, the design features an oval base (240 ft. long, 120 ft. wide) and no right angles other than those found on the stairs and in the temple at its summit, which towers 117 ft. above the surrounding city. The upward path consists of 121 steps, each just 6 in. wide, ascending at a steep 60° angle to the temple.

The Maya kept complex and accurate celestial calendars: the pyramid is perfectly aligned to face the setting sun on the date of the summer solstice, while nearby buildings point to positions in the sky (on key dates) of all the planets that the Maya knew. At a nearby ball court, a sacred game was played: the leader of the winning team would often be honored by ascending to the top of the pyramid to have his heart torn out with a piece of flint. Human sacrifice was a hallmark of Maya religion; some victims were decapitated, and their heads rolled down the stairs.

In the Maya language, *uxmal* means "thrice built," although there is evidence of five separate building periods, in keeping with the Maya's practice of erecting new structures on top of old ones. Maya legend holds that the pyramid was built in a single night by a dwarf magician who had been hatched from an egg by his witch mother. A more likely candidate is Uxmal's greatest King, Chan Chak K'ak'nal Ahaw, who ruled the city around A.D. 800 and erected many temples and palaces.

Historians cannot explain why Uxmal and other nearby Maya cities went into a sudden decline after A.D. 1200. The leading theory is that the two deities memorialized in the Pyramid of the Sorcerer, Itzamna (god of the sky) and Chac (god of rain) may have abandoned the Maya to a prolonged drought that strangled their culture. ■

VERBATIM
"[It was] a large, populous and highly civilized city. What led to its abandonment, no man can tell."
—John Lloyd Stephens, 1843

STEVE MCCURRY—MAGNUM PHOTOS

ROBERT FRERCK—ROBERT HARDING

GOING UP Adorning the sides of the Pyramid of the Sorcerer are dozens of representations of the rain god, Chac, above. At the pyramid's summit, the doorway to the temple is designed to resemble the open jaws of a huge Cosmic Serpent, in the form of the Maya god of the sky, Itzamna

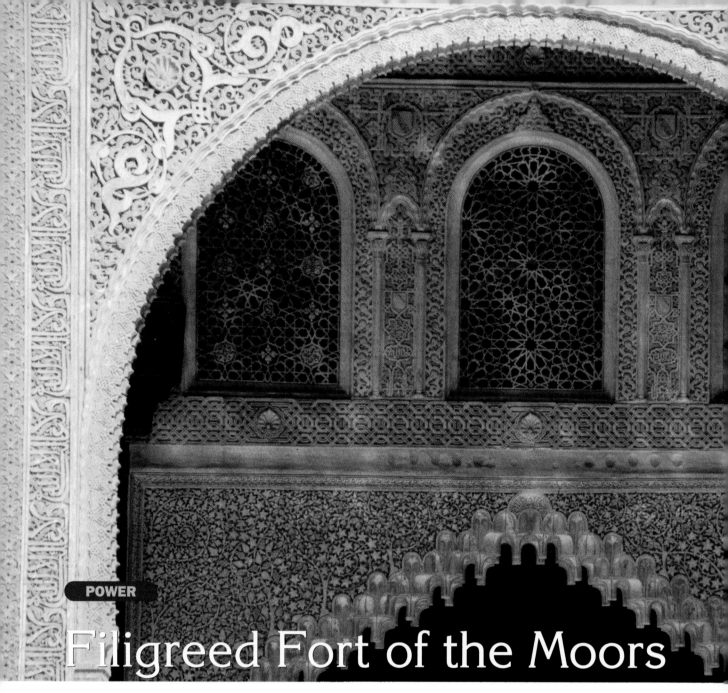

JED & KAORY SHARE-GETTY IMAGES

POWER

Filigreed Fort of the Moors

Intricate in artistry and grand in vision, the **Palace of the Alhambra** bears witness to the early influence of a Muslim aesthetic on the culture of Europe

NESTLED AMONG THE TALLEST MOUNTAINS IN SPAIN, just outside Granada, is an exquisite palace-cum-fortress that represents the high-water mark of Islamic architectural achievement in Western Europe. The Alhambra (Arabic for "Red Castle," a nod to the tint of the clay in its bricks) was built by a succession of Moorish kings in the Nasrid dynasty, beginning with Muhammad I in the 13th century. They created a wholly original architectural form, now known as caliphal style, that expresses the standard Moorish repertoire of arches, columns and domes in a new, intricately refined way that remains unique in the Islamic world. The Alhambra's towers, courtyards and lavishly decorated interior rooms flow gracefully, almost fluidly into one another, creating an organic whole in which the wood and stone almost seem to breathe.

Within these walls, temporal power is not flaunted; rather, spiritual power is evoked, even wooed. Nowhere is this truer than in the interior courtyards, which feature serene rows of slender columns, gently burbling fountains and reflecting pools that induce a sense of otherworldly calm. The greatest of these, the Court of Lions, with its graceful arcades set atop 124 white marble columns, flouts the Koran's prohibition of figurative imagery (there are numerous reliefs of animals and plants) to create a vision of paradise as limned by Arab poets. To Muslims, this palace is more than just a place of beauty and a piece of history: it is a physical manifestation of Allah's presence in this world. In 1492, when Boabdil, the last Nasrid king, relinquished Granada to the armies of Catholic Spain, legend has it that he turned to gaze at his enchanted citadel one last time, then fell to his knees and wept. ∎

INNER VISIONS Inside the Alhambra, graphic and written references to the next world abound. The magnificent Ambassador's Room, the largest in the complex, features a cedar ceiling inlaid with gold and etched with references to the seven heavens of Islamic theology. The Alhambra's builders viewed empty wall space as a canvas crying out for artistic attention: graceful geometric patterns, endlessly repeated, and delicately carved calligraphy of Islamic poetry and verses from the Koran cover almost every square inch of surface on the walls and ceilings. Small windows foster a dappled interplay of light and shadow

FERDINANDO SCIANNA·MAGNUM PHOTOS

PAOLO DALMASSO·GAMMA

TERRY WILLIAMS·GETTY IMAGES

PAUL TRUMMER·GETTY IMAGES

POWER

JONATHAN BLAIR—CORBIS

LEGACY OF BLOOD British royals often sought sanctuary at the tower, but they might have been safer outside its walls. King Henry VI was murdered on this site in 1471; Edward V, 13, and his brother, Richard, 10, vanished after being sent to the tower by their uncle Richard III in 1483. The skeletons of two children, apparently dating from this era, were uncovered beneath a stairwell in 1674. In the 1530s and '40s, two of Henry VIII's wives, Anne Boleyn and Catherine Howard, were beheaded here, as was Henry's closest adviser, Sir Thomas More. The White Tower, oldest section of the complex, is in the foreground

A Historic Chamber of Horrors

Job One for William the Conqueror: subdue English arms on the battlefield. Job Two: subdue English minds with a symbol of subjugation, the **Tower of London**

I F WILLIAM THE CONQUEROR, WHO BEGAN ERECTING THE Tower of London in 1066, had been able to see all that would transpire there over the next 900 years, he might have packed up and returned to France. His London keep has variously served as a royal residence, a records warehouse, a zoo, a prison, a place of execution for two English Queens (and the site of the secret murders of one King, one duke and two princes), a royal mint, a home to the crown jewels and, most recently, a magnet for itinerary-dazed, camera-toting tourists.

As it was, William needed an impressive (and impregnable) fortification to clinch his strategic chokehold over London. Within months of taking power, he began work on a modest stone enclosure along the banks of the Thames, within a corner of the old Roman city walls. A few years later, he completed the first version of his massive White Tower, a lofty medieval skyscraper fashioned by Norman masons from French stone. At 118 ft., the tower was like nothing William's stunned subjects had ever seen before; it dominated London both physically and psychologically. In the centuries that followed, the site expanded into a vast complex that included moats, fortified walls, additional towers and a palace. For the first six centuries of its history, the tower never quite shook off its first purpose, as a redoubt to which English royals could retreat in times of unrest. Nearly every British King, from William to the doomed Charles I, would take refuge in the tower during his reign. William the Conqueror used the words "vast and fierce" to describe the London populace his tower kept out— but the phrase perhaps better suits the fortress itself. ∎

Designed To Kill–and To Thrill

Named for the elegant white heron, **Shirasagijo Castle** captures the conflicting impulses of Japan's master builders, who clad even their redoubts in serene beauty

MIKE YAMASHITA-WOODFIN CAMP

O N A HILL OVERLOOKING A VERDANT JAPANESE PLAIN 25 miles west of Osaka stands the most peaceful-looking military fortification in the world. Shirasagijo ("White Heron Castle"), so named because its graceful, undulating lines recall the profile of the long-stemmed shorebird, is sometimes called Himeji Castle, for the city it overlooks.

Completed in just nine years (beginning in 1601) by 50,000 pairs of hands, Shirasagijo was built to serve as a regional stronghold for the Tokugawa Shogunate. One of the very few and best-preserved examples of 17th century fortress architecture that have survived to modern times, Himeji demonstrates that Japan's medieval architects couldn't stop themselves from creating beautiful, elegant structures—even when the building's purpose was grimly utilitarian. Vertical slits in the castle's façade appear intended to allow a summer breeze to circulate within, but their real purpose was to permit archers to shoot at enemy soldiers below. Elegant spouts at the corners of the castle's successive rooftops look like sculpted rain gutters, but were shaped to assist in pouring boiling oil onto besieging troops. A serpentine maze of sunken walkways (the only way to approach the base of the castle) seems designed to channel visitors past beautiful gardens but was actually intended to slow invaders, mak-

ing them vulnerable to attack from above. Himeji was also built to resist an assault of another kind: two massive wooden columns reaching from its foundation to the top of the donjon stabilize the structure in the event of an earthquake.

Surrounded by three concentric moats and soaring 150 ft. into the air, Himeji would be the indispensable objective for an invader who wished to control the area. But whether because it presented too daunting an obstacle to its enemies or because Japan's poet warriors could not bear to destroy something so beautiful, this most serene structure of war never saw a single battle. ■

Rise and Fall of a Hunting Lodge

Louis XIV, the "Sun King," is the presiding spirit of Versailles. Although he technically ascended to the throne of France in 1643 at age 4, he truly took power after the death of his regent, Cardinal Mazarin, in 1661. In the remaining 54 years of his reign, Louis became the most absolute of monarchs, and he shrewdly used the Château de Versailles as a symbol—and tool—of his power. Louis XIV, left, officially moved his royal residence from the Louvre in Paris to Versailles in 1682, far from the struggling masses in the city, whose 1648-53 uprising, termed La Fronde, had deeply worried the young King. Louis effectively used Versailles as a vast stage set in which he cowed and defanged his nobles. Once rivals in power to the monarchy, dukes and duchesses were reduced to bit players at Versailles, vying for favor in an endless quadrille of court fashion, court favor and court etiquette.

The exterior of the château is a bit dull; it is the interiors and extensive gardens that make this one of earth's most memorable places. The lavish Hall of Mirrors, right, designed by Louis XIV's chief architects, Jules Hardouin-Mansart and Charles Le Brun, reflects a society in which appearance was all.

But appearances could deceive: in her small chalet, Le Petit Trianon, King Louis XVI's wife Marie Antoinette created a facsimile of rural life where she and her attendants played at being milkmaids. Such charades came to an end on Oct. 6, 1789, when enraged peasants stormed the grounds. Marie Antoinette and her husband lost their heads on the guillotine in 1793.

But history was not finished with Versailles: more than a century later, diplomats from scores of countries gathered here in the wake of World War I—and for one last time, the map of Europe was redrawn in the halls of the Sun King.

ARCHIVO ICONOGRAFICO, S.A.—CORBIS (2)

ART SEITZ—GAMMA

THE CHÂTEAU DE VERSAILLES IS BOTH EXHILARATING and appalling: a symbol of France's cultural greatness, it is also a monument to oppression. But dig deep enough, and it's a weekend cabin on steroids. The palace, which reached an apogee of excess in the decades preceding the French Revolution, began as a simple hunting lodge. Here, in the countryside some 20 miles outside the Paris of his day, King Louis XIII would retreat from the burdens of court life to enjoy the hunt. In 1624 he built a modest lodge on the spot, and from that seed this most lavish of royal palaces grew … and grew … and grew. In 1631, Louis XIII added an eight-room château to the site. But it was his son and heir, Louis XIV, who was the visionary of Versailles. He added

BRUNO BARBEY—MAGNUM PHOTOS

POWER

The Sun King's Stage Set

You say you want a revolution? A visit to Louis XIV's monument to excess, the **Château de Versailles,** may leave you sharpening your guillotine

on to the château three times and lavished attention on its extensive formal gardens, which were designed by master landscape architect Andre le Notre. By 1682, Louis XIV was so smitten with his creation (and its safe remove from urban strife) that he moved his entire court to Versailles: the onetime retreat from power's burdens was now power's epicenter.

Here three Louises—XIV, XV and XVI—conducted business and pleasure amid formalized courtly rituals that turned everyday life into royal performance art: hundreds of standing courtiers would gather in the queen's antechamber simply to watch the royal family dine. The increasingly elaborate palace and gardens were justified as representing the splendor of the nation, and in truth, diplomats and other visitors

who clapped wondering eyes upon the place must have left marveling at the riches of the Sun King's realm.

Built to impress, this royal residence is all about its inventory. So here goes: at its height; some 1,000 French nobles lived at Versailles, attended to by 6,000 servants. The longest wing of the edifice stretches for a quarter-mile; there were 200 pieces of solid-silver furniture, including the Sun King's 8-ft. throne. If you find yourself somewhat nauseated by the unrelenting excess of it all, imagine how the overtaxed and underrepresented subjects of the French kings must have felt: by one estimate, half of France's annual revenue went to keeping up Versailles. Four different kings poured a nation's riches into this royal demesne—until the bill came due in 1789. ■

Designed to Fit the Future

More than six decades in construction, the **U.S. Capitol** wasn't built to the measure of a young republic, but it matches the size of its dreams

STANDING IN THE MARYLAND WILDERNESS THAT WAS to become the District of Columbia, Pierre Charles L'Enfant scouted a promontory known in the 1790s as Jenkins' Hill, which he described as "a pedestal waiting for a monument." The monument he planned to erect there, the U.S. Capitol Building, was, L'Enfant repeatedly claimed, already designed. Asked to produce the drawings, he demurred, saying they were stored "in his head." After the newborn Federal Government dismissed the irascible Frenchman, a design competition that promised $500 and one city lot to the winner settled on the neoclassical plan drawn up by a Scottish physician, portrait painter and steamboat engineer living in the British West Indies who dabbled in architecture in his spare time. William Thornton's Palladian design for two rectangular wings connected by a central dome drew praise from George Washington for its "grandeur, simplicity and con-venience." Thornton's design reflected the views of Washington's Federalist Party, allocating vast ceremonial space beneath a huge dome to palatial offices for a king-like President. It was only after Washington's death in 1799 that the much more populist ideals of Democratic-Republican Thomas Jefferson and his follow-

VERBATIM
"If people see the Capitol going on,
it is a sign we intend the Union to go on."
—Abraham Lincoln

GEORGES DEKEERLE—GETTY IMAGES

CORBIS

ers took hold. Under a new architect, Benjamin Latrobe, the Rotunda at the building's heart became, in Jefferson's words, "a hall of the people." The immense structure, whose dome stands 288 ft. high and shelters 16 acres and more than 500 rooms, is constantly being rebuilt, restored, redesigned and expanded. Like the country it stands for, it is always a work in progress. ∎

NEW VIEW: The main picture shows the West Front of the Capitol, the last section of its exterior still exposed to the world. Construction began in 1793 and continued through the War of 1812, when the British burned the partially completed building, along with much of Washington. President Abraham Lincoln ordered work to continue during the Civil War, above. The great dome and bronze Statue of Freedom that caps it were completed in 1863

POWER

Properly Perpendicular

Proudly pinnacled and pickled in pomp, the Palace of Westminster is the home of Britain's Parliament and the repository of its heritage

JOSÉ FUSTE—RAGA/CORBIS

WHETHER SWADDLED IN A DICKENSIAN FOG OR gleaming golden in the rays of the setting sun, the Palace of Westminster, home of Britain's Parliament, indelibly embodies the culture of the people it represents. Here, amid the ornate walls and lofty spires, the stained-glass windows and royal Robing Room, in the shadow of centuries-old Big Ben, a visitor feels immersed in the great saga of British history: turning a corner, one might expect to bump into Disraeli, Gladstone or Churchill. But the most remarkable aspect of this ancient structure ... is that it isn't ancient. Nor is Big Ben "centuries old"—it dates to 1858.

When the venerable House of Parliament, situated on the same enviable site along the Thames, burned to the ground in 1834, it offered Britons a chance to erect a new home for the House of Commons and House of Lords that reflected the nation's history. The committee charged with choosing an ar-

WRIT LARGE: The great edifice is dominated by two towers. The highest spire is the Victoria Tower, through which British monarchs make their ceremonial entrance into Parliament. At the other end of the complex is Big Ben, left, the mighty clock tower whose face, 20 ft. across, has become London's most indelible symbol. How big is Big Ben? So big that the tip of its 14-ft. hollow copper minute hand travels at the rate of a foot per minute. And how big is the entire Palace of Westminster complex? The riverfront face is 800 ft. long, and the building contains 1,180 rooms, 126 staircases and some two miles of corridors

VERBATIM
"[It] should be adapted to the Gothic origin ... of our constitution from a time when classic architecture was unknown in this country"
—Parliament's brief to designers

chitect made a critical decision: the building must not be designed along classical or neoclassical lines—British M.P.s should not convene behind the columns or beneath the dome of a "pagan" structure. The winning design, in a Gothic Revival style whose strong perpendicular elements were drawn from British cathedrals, was the work of Charles Barry.

The interiors of the immense edifice seem aged, like a good Scotch, in vats of pomp and circumstance. The eccentric Au-

gustus Pugin, an advocate and master of the Victorian Gothic style, labored for years on the details, sketching everything from floor tiles and coal buckets to doorknobs and inkstands. And though a newcomer, the building now bears history's scars: the House of Commons was destroyed by German bombs in 1941. At Prime Minister Winston Churchill's suggestion, it was rebuilt at too small a size to hold all its members at once, in order to retain its intimate feel. ■

Starting from Scratch

What an opportunity—to conjure a city out of thin air. But though Brazil's capital, **Brasília,** looks great at a distance, it needs a heart transplant

Cathedral (under construction), 1967

City Center

Foreign Ministry

Congress Building

PHOTO CREDITS, CLOCKWISE FROM TOP LEFT: BETTMANN CORBIS; JAMES DAVIS-EYE UBIQUITOUS-CORBIS; YANN ARTHUS-BERTRAND-CORBIS; BETTMANN CORBIS

IF THE FUTURE THAT MODERNISM PROMISED—BUT NEVER quite delivered—has an address, it's a dusty savanna in the Brazilian state of Goiás, more than 500 miles from the nation's cultural center, Rio de Janeiro. Brazil's President Juscelino Kubitschek decided in 1955 to relocate the country's capital city to this uninhabited wasteland, a tabula rasa upon which it could sketch the future with a free hand. An idealized tomorrow was just around the corner, he believed, if he could just build the right structures to house it.

The Swiss-French prophet of Modernism Le Corbusier dreamed of demolishing Paris and replacing its Beaux-Arts chaos with miles of neatly ordered, evenly spaced tower blocks. At last, this ideal city seemed within reach, if not that of the grid-entranced "Corbu" himself, then those of his pupil, Brazilian architect Oscar Niemeyer (who designed the buildings), in partnership with Lucio Costa (who mapped out the master plan for the new city) and Roberto Burle Marx (a landscape designer who created the numerous grand outdoor spaces). The city they created looked magnificent in sketches, appears striking but slightly less wonderful in photographs and nearly sucks the life out of the people doomed to live in its buildings and walk its streets.

Because the use of names reeked of the past, everything in Brasília is designated with a number—not only the streets but also blocks, buildings and entire neighborhoods. Because in the future everyone would drive, Brasília has no traffic lights or street corners. These antiques are replaced by a flowing lattice of express lanes, feeder roads and traffic circles that loop through and around buildings. Because walking would soon be passé, there are no sidewalks or crossing lanes (giving pedestrians good reason to fear for their lives), and almost none of the buildings are located within convenient walking distance of the others. Gentlemen, start your engines!

To be fair, many of the designs exhibit a breathtaking, if bloodless, beauty. Niemeyer's Alvorada Palace, the presidential mansion, appears to float above delicate tapering columns. And all the structures impress with their big, bold shapemaking: a theater in the form of a pyramid, a cathedral with a resplendent stained-glass ceiling that reminds some viewers of an inverted chalice or a crown of thorns, a Congress Building that looks, well, a bit like a glass harmonica. Brasília is a collection of virtuoso objects jumbled together without any of the connective organic tissue that forges space into a community. The city's stance toward the power of government seems designed to invite awe rather than involvement. It takes a heap of livin' to make a blueprint into a home—and Brasília's got a heap of livin' ahead of it. ∎

A Translucent Dome Is a New

Like its war-torn nation, Germany's **Reichstag** had been burned, bombed and

FOR 28 YEARS THE SYMBOL OF GERMANY'S DIVISION AFter World War II was, appropriately, a barrier: the Berlin Wall traced a 26-mile gash through the center of the nation's capital city. After the Wall fell in 1989, the legislators of the newly united nation met in Bonn, capital of West Germany. But in 1991 the members of the Bundestag decided to return the seat of government to Berlin and create a symbol of national union by restoring the historic capitol building, the Reichstag. In an ironic twist of history, a British architect, Norman Foster, won an international competition to bring the building back to life for the 21st century.

Designed in a neoclassical style by German architect Paul Wallot and completed in 1894, the bulky, boxy Reichstag bore the wounds of Germany's recent history. In 1933 Adolf Hitler's accomplices burned the building and blamed the deed on communists, assisting the Nazi leader's rise to power. Beginning in 1943 the Reichstag was bombed by Allied planes; in 1945, victorious Russian soldiers vandalized it after Hitler's downfall. In a final insult, vandals of a different kind—East German designers—"restored" the building's interior on the cheap in the late 1960s and early '70s.

Foster's mission was not only to bring the building back to life but also to make it embody the hopes and ideals of the newly united nation. Wallot's building had sported a bulky cupola of steel and glass, which echoed the shape of a Prussian helmet. When legislators insisted the dome be rebuilt, Foster initially opposed the idea. But then he embraced it—and transformed it with the sort of high-tech flourish that is his trademark. The translucent dome doesn't merely squat on the building; it opens it up. The inverted, mirrored cone at its center channels light deep into the legislative chamber several stories beneath: literally shedding light on the work of the politicians, it acts as a brilliant design metaphor for the transparency of democracy. But the view it offers is not only into the building: the spiral walkways along the hemisphere's circumference offer transfixed visitors spectacular views of Berlin. (*For an interior view of the dome, see the following portfolio.*)

In keeping with the theme of opening up the building to scrutiny, Foster and his team pre-

STREET LEVEL Seen from the street at night, the dome gleams like a beacon, a brilliant synthesis of Germany's past and future. A giant sun shield—solar-powered, of course—follows the path of the sun around the dome on bright days, reducing heat and glare

JEREMY WALKER—THE IMAGE BANK—GETTY IMAGES

JOHN D. NORMAN—CORBIS

Crown For a United Germany

vandalized—until a British architect's "fiat lux" banished the darkness

served some of the hundreds of graffiti messages left by Russian soldiers in 1945 and later covered up by wallboard. "Our approach was radical, based in the view that the history of the building should not be sanitized," Foster told the New York *Times* in 1999. But the reborn Reichstag looks to the future as well as the past: Foster designed the building to use as little energy as possible. The dome brings solar heat into the structure, while its power plant burns clean, efficient rapeseed oil. The ventilation system is also natural. The old Reichstag, heated and cooled by fossil fuels, produced 7,000 tons of carbon dioxide a year. The redesigned building's CO_2 emissions have dropped 94%, to 440 tons a year. When it comes to readapting historic buildings for a modern era, Foster's Reichstag is a clear winner. ∎

The Norman Conquest

Long the high priest of high tech, Norman Foster is now breathing new life into old buildings and designing a greener future for cities

NOVELIST AYN RAND WAS INSPIRED BY FRANK LLOYD Wright when she created the larger-than-life character of Howard Roark, the genius form giver of *The Fountainhead*. Were she living today, Rand might find an even better exemplar of the architect as heroic, self-made individualist in the person of Britain's Norman Foster. Seventy in 2004, the designer isn't content to bestride the architectural world like a colossus; rather, he hurls himself across it like a modern-day Mercury—deity of speed and commerce—as he moves among his offices in London, Hong Kong, Frankfurt, Berlin, Paris, Riyadh and Tokyo. He flies jets, drives a Porsche, competes in the marathon. On his drawing board, entire city centers are reduced

to rubble, then given new form. He has designed London bridges, Spanish subways, Asian airports, Italian furniture. He has shaped city halls, aircraft museums, lavish yachts. Knighted by Queen Elizabeth in 1990, Lord Foster of Thames Bank has brilliantly reinvented both the British Museum (by covering up its courtyard) and Berlin's Reichstag (by opening up its roof). Long a high priest of high tech, he was once asked to name the perfect building—and cited the Boeing 747.

Foster is no child of privilege: he was born into a working-class family in 1935 in Manchester and left school at 16 to work in the city treasurer's office, then served a term in the Royal Air Force. He returned to toil as a contracts manager in an architect's office and enrolled in the architecture school at the University of Manchester at age 21. His great leap forward came in the form of a fellowship for postgraduate study at Yale University; he claims he "discovered himself" in America's expansiveness, drive and promise.

At Yale, Foster roomed with fellow Briton Richard Rodgers, who shared his interest in the aesthetic that would later be dubbed high tech: the use of unfinished materials and advanced technology, the inside-out exposure of infrastructure,

the delight in form and movement. The two returned to England and founded the firm of Team Four with their architect wives; their first big project was an electronics factory (since demolished), a perfect commission for their emerging industrial style. After the partnership folded for lack of work, Foster's elegant design for an insurance headquarters in Ipswich made waves, and he found himself in demand.

Deep in the genetic code of the former airman's buildings is a feeling for hangar-like lightness and strength, along with frugality of consumption. A good example is his 1981 design for the airport at Stansted, England. Earlier airports had massive concentrations of ductwork above their ceilings for air conditioning, lighting and electrical services; Foster realized huge savings in structural mass and energy consumption by shifting the utilities underground, leaving a floating roof and walls that could open to natural daylight. Most major airports built since have followed his innovations.

The ideal of humane efficiency, understood as social responsibility, undergirds much of Foster's work. In Frankfurt's Commerzbank, he built a supertower that blooms with garden atriums and uses natural ventilation (vs. fuel-gobbling air conditioning) for 60% of the year. Innovative "sunscoops" funnel natural light into many of his buildings.

Though long identified with futuristic design, Foster in recent years has learned to meld the best of past and present. When the British Museum's library moved to massive new premises, it left behind one of the great English spaces: the 1857 Round Reading Room designed by Sydney Smirke, whose shallow dome was surrounded by a two-acre internal court. Foster saved the masterpiece by sweeping away the clutter of old book-stack buildings from around it and covering the court with a light-welcoming roof. In similar fashion, his renovation of Berlin's Reichstag left large sections of the historic building untouched, while he revitalized the entire structure by crowning it with a transparent dome.

Foster may have missed his Howard Roark moment, but he does have a fictional doppelgänger: Philip Kerr's thriller *Gridiron* (1994) features a famous, ego-driven British architect who ends up being squashed to death in one of his own sentient (if grouchy) buildings. Fair enough, but one suspects the architect would have preferred that the Foster imposter be cooked to death by sentient (if grumpy) sunscoops. ∎

CAROLYN DJANOGLY–AURORA PHOTOS; INSET: PAWELL LIBERIA–CORBIS

VERBATIM
"[Foster insists] that the poetics
of a building must grow out of its legible,
fully expressed structure."
—Robert Hughes

British Museum Courtyard

Commerzbank Building

PORTFOLIO: Norman Foster

Chek Lap Kok Airport

COMMERZBANK BUILDING, FRANKFURT, 1997 A milestone in environmental design, the building is the world's greenest skyscraper. Nine three-story gardens bloom at various levels of the 984-ft. structure (Europe's tallest), which has a 12-story garden atrium at its heart. Office windows open to let in natural air, and toilets flush with "gray" water from cooling towers. Water-filled grids in ceilings cool offices in summer, while solar power helps heat them in winter.

BRITISH MUSEUM COURTYARD, LONDON, 2003 Foster saved the museum library's vintage Reading Room and created a vast entrance area by stripping away a jumble of storage buildings that encircled the structure and covering the courtyard with a steel-and-glass roof. Some call Foster's work sterile; British writer Will Self said of this space: "Never has a finished building looked so much like its computer visualization."

CHEK LAP KOK AIRPORT, HONG KONG, 1998 The world's largest airport—Foster calls it a "horizontal cathedral"—was built on an artificial island. Inside, he enclosed 125 acres under one roof to create the world's largest single room, the size of more than 100 football fields.

❝High-tech is misleading ... You can't separate technology from the

Reichstag

REICHSTAG BUILDING, BERLIN, 1999 Foster's spiral ramp resembles the interior of Frank Lloyd Wright's Guggenheim Museum in New York City. The transparent dome offers views across united Berlin, while the cone of mirrored glass at its center diffuses and reflects natural light deep into the building's cavernous interior, illuminating the workings of the legislators.

MILLENNIUM BRIDGE, LONDON, 2000 When the bridge was opened, enormous crowds flocked to cross it—and the roadway began wobbling. It was closed and additional structural support was added, while British tabloids jeered, dubbing Foster "Lord Wobbly." Foster is remaking modern London: he will remodel Trafalgar Square and has new buildings on the drawing board for Canary Wharf and the City.

Millennium Bridge

BRITISH MUSEUM: IAN BERRY—MAGNUM PHOTOS; HONG KONG AIRPORT: PAUL HU—ASSIGNMENT ASIA; COMMERCE BANK: FRANK SEIFERT—THE IMAGE BANK—GETTY; REICHSTAG INTERIOR OF DOME: PAUL HAHN/LAIS-AURORA PHOTOS; MILLENNIUM BRIDGE: PAWEL LIBERA—CORBIS

humanistic, spiritual content of a building. **"** —Norman Foster

Where We Worship

God that made the world ... dwelleth not in temples made with hands," St. Paul wrote to early Christians in Rome. Perhaps not, but surely a sense of the divine can be found in our houses of worship, which reflect the many ways in which we seek transcendence. Like Angkor Wat, some of them aspire, with towers soaring upward. Others chastise, sober and severe. And some awe with sheer size. But almost all of them share one principle of design: sunlight is our best metaphor for divine illumination

GLENN ALLISON—GETTY IMAGES

ANGKOR WAT, CAMBODIA
Now a Buddhist shrine, the vast complex was begun in the 12th century as a center of Hindu religion and culture

THE GLORY THAT WAS ... The mural above, featured at the Tournaire Museum at Delphi, captures the precarious topography of the sacred site, where temples and treasuries cling to the hillside. The large building at the center is the Temple of Apollo. While the bleached stone of these ruins suggests to modern eyes a purity and simplicity we often mistakenly regard as classical, the Greeks in fact painted their buildings in bright colors—a point overlooked by the muralist

ROSSI XAVIER GAMM

The Navel of Planet Earth

The ancient Greeks, bearing gifts, climbed the steep slopes of Mount Parnassus to reach the site sanctified by a prophetic Oracle: **Delphi**

ZEUS, RESOLVED TO FIND THE CENTER OF THE WORLD, released two sacred eagles from the ends of the earth. The place where they met, a spring on the southern slopes of Mount Parnassus, was deemed to be the omphalos—the navel of the earth. It was here that the ancient Greeks built a temple to Apollo (on what may have been an earlier Mycenaean cult site) in the 8th century B.C. Greeks seeking divine guidance would journey from all the city-states to Delphi, climbing 2,000 ft. to visit the Oracle, where a priestess would inhale the intoxicating vapors that issued from a cave on the site and answer questions in cryptic verse. The Oracle's cave is lost to history; archaeologists believe it may have been covered over by landslides.

Because Delphi was sacred to all Greeks, the site was nominally independent (in truth, it changed hands among several city-states many times over the centuries) and incorporated a striking variety of Greek architectural styles. Treasury buildings to house donations were built in the Ionic and Doric styles of the Siphnians and Athenians, respectively. The Chians erected an altar of contrasting black and white marble; its stoa (porch) had seven fluted columns, each cut from a single stone. At the center of the complex stood the Temple of Apollo; the shrine pictured here is the Tholos, believed to be dedicated to the earth goddess, Gaia.

The greatest questions confronting the Greeks were asked of the Oracle. Should Croesus invade Persia? He was assured that if he did, he would topple a great empire—but realized too late that the empire he destroyed might be his own. Who was the wisest philosopher? The priestess said Socrates. He humbly disagreed and tried to prove the Oracle wrong by searching Athens for a teacher wiser than himself. Unable to find one, he reluctantly endorsed the Oracle's choice. And how should the Athenians fight the invading army of Xerxes? The prophecy that "the wooden wall only shall not fail" was interpreted to mean that the city should be abandoned and the invading Persians should be confronted on the water—in the Athenian fleet of fast-moving wooden boats—rather than on land. In this, the Oracle proved especially prescient: the Greek victory at Salamis is regarded as one of history's greatest naval battles. ∎

ROBERT EVERTS·STONE·GETTY IMAGES

SPRINGDALE PUBLIC LIBRARY
405 S. PLEASANT ST
SPRINGDALE, AR 72764

Epicenter of Empires

Built by the Romans, sacred to the Byzantines, conquered by Christian Crusaders and then by Muslim sultans, **Hagia Sophia** bestrides history

ONE OF THE WORLD'S GREAT WITNESSES OF HISTORY, Hagia Sophia (Divine Wisdom) straddles cultures, empires, faiths and continents. For 1,000 years it was Christianity's foremost church; for 500 years it was one of Islam's chief mosques. Desanctified in the 1930s, it endures as a museum. It is built squarely upon one of civilization's fault lines, high on a hill in Istanbul, formerly Constantinople. Look east, and you see the Bosporus, where Asia and Europe collide. Look west, and you see boats plying the Sea of Marmara, which links Istanbul to the Mediterranean. Look inside the doors of the great edifice, and you are peering into another dimension: time. This building was 1,000 years old when St. Peter's was built in Rome. It was 600 years old when the spires of Chartres Cathedral survived a devastating fire. One of the great functioning relics of the Roman Empire, it was built by the Emperor Justinian beginning in A.D. 532, some 80 years after Constantinople was founded as the capital of Rome's eastern realm by the Emperor Constantine, who made Christianity the official religion of the empire. Some 11,000 stonemasons labored to complete the structure in five years. "O Solomon, I have excelled thee!" Justinian is said to have exclaimed when the task was done.

The wonder of Hagia Sophia is its mighty dome: 107 ft. in diameter, its circular base is pierced by 40 windows. The effect is of the dome floating in the clouds, suspended in the air. The two Greek architect-engineers who built it solved intricate geometric challenges in supporting a huge dome upon a

SURVIVOR For 1,000 years Constantinople reigned as the capital of Rome's eastern empire, which became the Byzantine Empire, but in 1453 Sultan Mehmet II conquered the city for Islam. The tolerant ruler preserved Hagia Sophia from desecration, saving its historic mosaics by plastering over them. Muslims erected four minarets around the building and placed a crescent moon on the dome, sanctifying it as a mosque

square base. Attached exterior half-domes bear part of its weight, much like the flying buttresses of Gothic cathedrals.

The fault lines beneath the building are more than fanciful; it has withstood dozens of major earthquakes, the first of them while Justinian was still living, in 558. The great dome collapsed, and the Emperor ordered it rebuilt—with the dome raised 20 ft. higher. After Christianity divided into Western Roman and Eastern Orthodox branches in 1054, Constantinople was conquered and ransacked in 1204, in the Fourth Crusade. European knights rode their horses into the building but were restrained from desecrating it. When Muslims conquered Constantinople in 1453, Sultan Mehmet II saw to it that the church was spared. It served as a mosque for nearly five centuries, until Kemal Ataturk, the Eurocentric creator of modern Turkey, turned it into a museum in 1934.

Desanctified by religion but ennobled by time, Hagia Sophia endures, surviving a bomb set off in its nave by Kurdish terrorists in 1994 and an earthquake that killed 13,000 in 1999. For once, the poet is wrong: Justinian could very well boast, "Look upon my work, ye mighty—and prepare." ■

TOP LEFT: ROBERT FRERCK—WOODFIN CAMP; TOP RIGHT: ROBERT FRERCK—ODYSSEY/CHICAGO; OPPOSITE: ERICH LESSING/ART RESOURCE

VERBATIM
"Its interior is not
illuminated from without by the sun … the
radiance comes into being within it."
—Procopius

WORSHIP

Sacred City in the Jungle

Built by a Khmer king in the 12th century, the great temple complex of **Angkor Wat** has been sacred to two religions—but its future is imperiled

PAUL CHESLEY—NATIONAL GEOGRAPHIC—GETTY IMAGES (2)

ENDANGERED Angkor Wat is listed as a World Heritage Site in Danger by UNESCO; it is threatened on three fronts. Although its buildings were not heavily bombed during 20th century fighting in Cambodia, they were hit by light mortar fire and scarred by machine-gun bullets, and the area was extensively mined. Impoverished Cambodians have learned that they can earn the equivalent of up to a year's wages by stripping ancient statuary from the site and selling it to smugglers. Even preservation efforts can be damaging: in the 1990s, well-intentioned Third World antiquities "experts" began scrubbing away centuries of dirt and vegetation with a caustic chemical cleaner that erased some of the original bas-relief detail from the stonework

ants, Angkor Wat seemed to the first Europeans who beheld it to be a vision from another world. Or at least another continent: when French colonial authorities displayed artifacts from the site in Paris, they pointed to the supposed influences of China, India and Egypt on its design, so sure were they that the "backward" people of Southeast Asia could never have produced such a marvel on their own.

They were wrong. The Khmer civilization that built Angkor Wat was enormously sophisticated, both in architecture and engineering. Here massive stone blocks are joined without mortar, forming permanent, stable bonds from their own weight. And the system of canals and moats surrounding Angkor Wat consists of nearly perfect straight lines, which in most cases deviate only inches from exact alignment over the course of several miles.

Built by King Suryavarman II beginning in the first half of the 12th century, the vast temple complex—it is nearly a mile long—is laid out to reflect the Hindu idea of the universe. Surrounding moats represent the oceans at the end of the world; the massive outer walls evoke the mountain ranges that separate the continents; the five towers at its center stand for the five peaks of Mount Meru, royal dwelling place of the Hindu gods. The towers recall lotus blossoms about to bloom, while galleries and corridors align with the points of the compass.

Angkor Wat housed as many 20,000 people on separate levels in its peak years: peasant workers on the bottom tier; rich merchants in the middle; and the King, with his ministers and priests, on the highest level. In later centuries the local population converted to Buddhism, and the giant statue of Vishnu in the central tower was replaced by a golden Buddha. Today, Angkor Wat is imperiled, yet it is so potent a symbol of national pride that its outline adorns the Cambodian flag. ■

ERECTED BY SOME ANCIENT MICHELANGELO, IT IS grander than anything left to us by Greece or Rome," wrote Henri Mouhot, the French explorer who visited Angkor Wat in 1861, becoming the first European to see Cambodia's sacred city. By then, the world's largest religious monument (its name means "Temple of the Capital") had been largely uninhabited—save for a few dozen Buddhist monks—for more than 400 years. Overrun with the creeping tentacles of strangler fig trees that resemble the fingers of gi-

UPKEEP The extensive complex is dotted with interior courtyards. Potala is still maintained by traditional Tibetan methods: the walls of the Red Palace are covered each year with a fresh coat of pigment by workers lowered from above on ropes made of yak hair

JOHN EASTCOTT-YVA MOMATIUK/UK-WOODFIN CAMP

JOHN EASTCOTT-YVA MOMATIUK-WOODFIN CAMP

WORSHIP

Tibet's Haunted Monastery

Monumental and majestic, **Potala Palace** is the spiritual home of every Tibetan, but its presiding deity, the Dalai Lama, hasn't seen it since 1959

POTALA PALACE, THE MOST STRIKING EXAMPLE OF CLASsic Tibetan architecture, is one of the few symbols of Tibetan nationalism that has survived the ongoing cultural purge by the Chinese, who have occupied the country since 1950. As befits the crowning jewel of a mountain kingdom, Potala ("sacred place") Palace sits on a high ridge located more than 10,000 ft. above sea level, surrounded by hills that ring a vast plain. Its site has been the home of Tibet's kings and monks since the 7th century.

In 1645, the fifth Dalai Lama commissioned the first section, the White Palace, to commemorate the return of the Tibetan capital to the the nearby city of Lhasa. After his death in 1682, a second section (the Red Palace) was built on top of the first. The completed structure towers 13 stories over the crest of the Marpo Ri (Red Hill) ridge and stretches almost a quarter-mile from north to south. Civil affairs are conducted in the lower White Palace, while religious matters are the province of the Red Palace above: in Tibet, spiritual authority trumps temporal power.

Among the most sacred and impressive precincts in the Red Palace are the tomb shrines (stupas) of eight deceased Dalai Lamas. The stupa of the fifth Dalai Lama is wrapped with 110,000 sheets of gold foil and inlaid with 18,677 pearls and gems, as well as coral, amber and agate. Reports of Lhasa and the palace reached European ears in the form of fables of a mythical Asian kingdom, Shangri-la. British photographer John Claude White astounded the world when he released the first pictures of the palace in 1904.

The building's gently tapering stone walls become thinner as they reach its top. Vast on every scale, the palace encloses more than a quarter-million square ft., contains some 1,000 rooms and is home to more than 200,000 statues and other artworks. But the building is no fairy-tale palace: the ascetic private chamber of the Dalai Lama (unused since he went into exile in 1959) is said to measure only 5 ft. on each side. ∎

CHINA TOURISM PRESS-THE IMAGE BANK-GETTY IMAGES

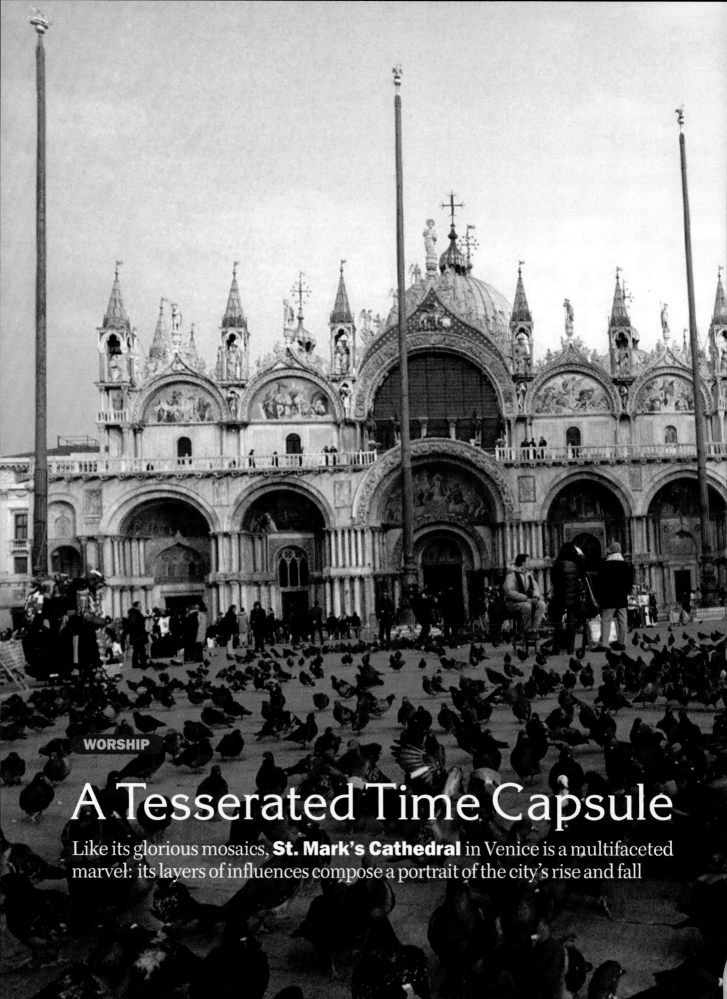

A Tesserated Time Capsule

Like its glorious mosaics, **St. Mark's Cathedral** in Venice is a multifaceted marvel: its layers of influences compose a portrait of the city's rise and fall

BENAINOUS—VANDEVILLE—GAMMA

SIMONE HUBER—STONE—GETTY IMAGES

VISIONS OF BYZANTIUM The massive rounded arches and windowed domes of St. Mark's reveal its central influence, Hagia Sophia in today's Istanbul. The cathedral's 320-ft. red brick campanile, or bell tower (behind the inset picture, above), is one of its oldest components. Raised in A.D. 912, it stood for 990 years before it collapsed in 1902; it was rebuilt and reopened on its 1,000th anniversary, in 1912

BACKDROP TO MILLIONS OF TOURIST PICTURES AND prized perch for a piazza full of pigeons, St. Mark's Cathedral runs the danger of being taken for granted. Yet it is one of Europe's most historic structures, a living link to the days of the Crusades and to the emergence of the great merchant city-state of Venice as an imperial power. Originally a simple brick ducal chapel, it grew into one of the great symbols of Venice's wealth and influence after the body of St. Mark (San Marco) was smuggled out of Egypt by two Venetian traders in 1094. The building is a kaleidoscope of influences; it borrows elements from different cultures and eras—Byzantine, Romanesque, Gothic, Oriental, Renaissance—and yet achieves a unity all its own. Some of its treasures were not borrowed but pillaged: the four bronze horses that stand in a place of honor over the cathedral's portal were looted from Constantinople in 1204 in the Fourth Crusade.

The statues were cast in the 4th century A.D., either in Greece or Rome. They mark both Venice's rise to power and its final decline: after Napoleon conquered Venice in 1797, ending its days as an independent city-state, he shipped the horses to Paris. They were returned after his downfall in 1815. Endangered by pollution, the original bronzes were removed from the church in the late 1970s and now reside in a climate-controlled display area inside the church; those visible here against the window above the central doorway are copies.

The real glory of St. Mark's can be found within its walls, indeed *on* its walls: they are covered in more than an acre of rich, shimmering mosaics, derived from the Byzantine tradition. Greek artisans were brought to Venice in 1100 to begin creating the mosaics, whose individual pieces, or tesserae, are made of gold, marble and the luminous glass for which the city has been known for centuries. ∎

When Architecture Aspired

Soaring on the outside, radiant within, **Chartres Cathedral** and its Gothic kin across Europe are repositories of medieval spirituality and technology

SWEDISH FILMMAKER INGMAR BERGMAN INTRODUCED *The Seventh Seal*, his 1957 film set in the Middle Ages, by recalling the story of the great cathedral Nôtre Dame du Chartres: "There is an old story of how the cathedral of Chartres was struck by lightning and burned to the ground. Then thousands of people came from all points of the compass, like a giant procession of ants, and together they began to rebuild the cathedral on its old site. They worked until the building was completed—master builders, artists, laborers, clowns, noblemen, priests, burghers. But they all remained anonymous, and no one knows to this day who built the cathedral of Chartres."

Indeed, part of the enduring appeal of Europe's great Gothic cathedrals is their backstory: the great structures arose across northern Europe in a frenzy of devotion. Here was an age when new technologies fused with religious passion, and to build was to pray: between 1170 and 1270, some 80 cathedrals and 500 major churches were built in France alone.

So lasting is the spell of these sacred spaces that centuries later many cathedrals—St. Patrick's and St. John the Divine in Manhattan, the National Cathedral in Washington—were still being built on the Gothic template. Yet there is a whiff of the modern in these structures: they marry form to function. The technical breakthroughs that create their soaring, aspirational quality are in plain view: the Gothic arch, stronger and able to bear more weight than its rounded Romanesque predecessor; the stone rib vaults that ground the 121-ft.-tall ceilings;

the flying buttresses that support the high walls on the outside, creating the unprecedented height of the interior. Freed from bearing loads, the inner walls seem to disappear, replaced by enormous windows, stained-glass artworks that suffuse the nave with otherworldly hues. The effect? Liftoff.

The masterminds of the Gothic style were itinerant stonemasons—at once artists, architects and engineers—who moved across Europe, sharing their expertise through the apprentice system. How this cascade of fusions—between secular and sacred, art and science, mystic and mason, peasant and noble—must have appealed to Bergman, whose films limn a world of alienated, isolated souls, stripped of vision and purpose. ∎

SACRED GEOMETRIES
At Chartres, even the flying buttresses echo the Gothic arch that gives the building its height, while a spiral stairway might please a Frank Lloyd Wright or Norman Foster. Chartres was a pilgrimage destination where miraculous cures took place. Pilgrims followed another spiral— an inlaid labyrinth on the nave floor— as a form of religious observance

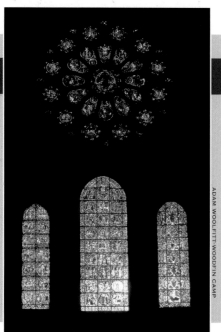

Core Sample of Medieval Life

Chartres Cathedral is the latest of a series of churches and temples that have been built on its site: religious observances here date to the time of the Druids, before Christianity came to France. In 1194 a Romanesque church occupied the site, and two great spires were being added as an entry portal. The church burned down, but the bases of the spires stood, and the townspeople erected the new cathedral in a span of only 20 to 30 years, making the building more focused in design than most Gothic churches, which can reflect stylistic evolutions that span centuries. However, Chartres' west front does reflect two different periods: the unadorned right spire dates from the late 12th century; the far more ornate left spire was completed in 1513. Chartres' great rose window is a pinnacle of stained-glass artistry; Abbot Suger (1081-1151), the designer-cleric who introduced the Gothic style at the church of St. Denis in Paris, believed that radiant light was the closest mankind could come to experiencing divine illumination.

VERBATIM
"Nothing can compare with Chartres. It is the very mind of the Middle Ages in visible form."
—Émile Mâle

MARC GARANGER·CORBIS

France's Citadel of Sanctity

Seemingly inviolate off the coast of Normandy, **Mont St. Michel** has still moved with history's tides—from the age of visions to the age of revolution

VICTOR HUGO CALLED IT "A MAJESTIC PYRAMID STANDING on a huge rock, shaped and carved by the Middle Ages." Pre-Christian legends held that it was the island where the souls of the dead congregated. But for Aubert, Bishop of nearby Avranches in the eighth century, the rocky crag off France's northern coast was a place to meditate. One day the Archangel Michael appeared to Aubert and commanded him to build a church. The idea was madness, Aubert insisted: the steep cliffs that ascended from the crashing surf and the treacherous tides that whipped around the island made the task impossible. But Michael persisted, appearing before Aubert two more times, even tapping him on the head for emphasis. (The bishop's preserved skull, complete with a dent made by the angry angel, is still on display in Avranches.)

The small chapel that Aubert began in the year 708 blossomed, through the centuries, into a complex of churches, monasteries, convents, and fortifications—jammed every-which-way onto an island less than 1 sq. mile in area. As more buildings were added, earlier structures became the foundations for newer edifices. Beginning in the year 966, Benedictine monks completely encircled the natural outcropping of rock that dominated the island with a series of dormitories and chapels, thus raising a level platform to the 200-ft. summit.

In the eleventh century, a new monastery, a Gothic masterpiece appropriately named La Merveille ("the Marvel") was perched atop the island. Throughout the Middle Ages, Mont St. Michel became both a place of pilgrimage and an unassailable strategic redoubt in wartime. What armies could not do, however, ideologues could: the monks were evicted during the French Revolution and Mont. St. Michel became a prison. It was not until 1966 (1,000 years after the founding of the Benedictine monastery on the island) that men of god were welcomed back to a place where an angel and a bishop once contended. ∎

ED FREEMAN—THE IMAGE BANK—GETTY IMAGES

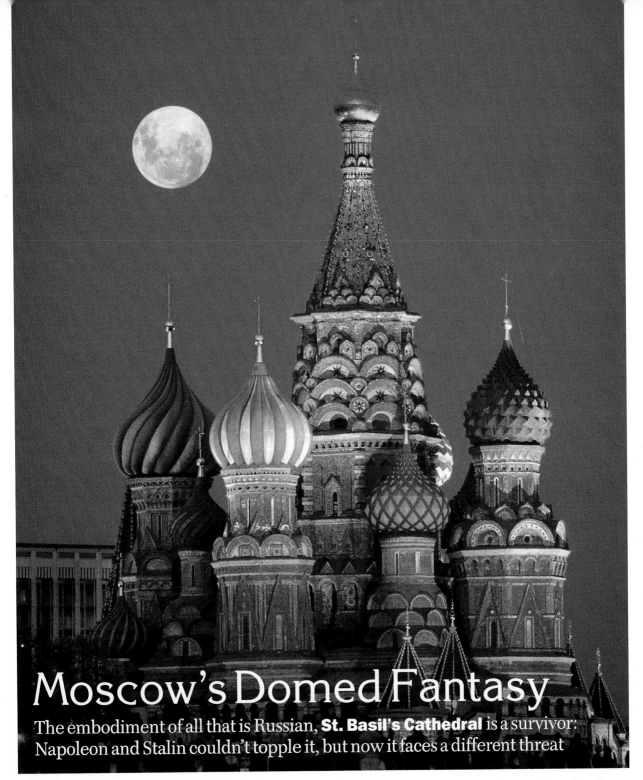

Moscow's Domed Fantasy

The embodiment of all that is Russian, **St. Basil's Cathedral** is a survivor: Napoleon and Stalin couldn't topple it, but now it faces a different threat

CHARLES O'REAR-CORBIS

FRESH FROM HIS 1552 VICTORY OVER THE MONGOLS AT Kazan, Czar Ivan (the Terrible) commanded that a new church be built outside the gates of the Kremlin, where all Moscow could see it. In designing the Cathedral of the Intercession (later known as St. Basil's, when the remains of the Russian holy man were interred there), architect Postnik Yakolev borrowed Romanesque, Gothic, and Renaissance motifs. But he topped it off with a uniquely Russian twist: a bouquet of nine wondrous domes, each a different size, shape and color from the others. The result is a riot of texture, hue and contour that—rather than being chaotic—achieves an unexpected harmony, drawing the eye of the viewer serenely toward the gold-plated dome that crowns the church's spire.

Napoleon ordered the church burnt down when he retreated from Moscow in 1812; his freezing troops failed to do so. Joseph Stalin—a czar of a different color—once considered demolishing St. Basil's to make room for a subway station. The architect he chose for the task threatened to cut his throat rather than carry out the order. When a disgruntled crowd of Muscovites gathered to support him, Stalin relented, but he dispatched the architect to the Gulag in revenge.

A different menace now imperils St. Basil's. In 2003 it was discovered that shifting soil under the cathedral is imperiling its stability. Preservation experts are now exploring ways to save the edifice that was built by one of history's greatest tyrants—and that two others tried, but failed, to destroy. ■

Holy, Roman And Imperial

Italy's vast **Basilica of St. Peter** is a testament to Renaissance genius

THE MILLIONS OF TOURISTS WHO PASS THROUGH THE doors of the Basilica of St. Peter in Vatican City each year are drawn by a trinity of reasons. Heirarchy plays a part: this is the primary church of Roman Catholicism, oldest and largest of Christian religions. Art and history are here as well: filled with the sublime works of Italy's High Renaissance, St. Peter's is home to Michelangelo's moving *Pièta* and hundreds of other treasures. Finally, visitors come to marvel at the sheer scale and grandeur of the place. It is Christendom's largest church, and should any unbeliever question its primacy, plaques marking the sizes of other churches are set in its marble floors for purposes of comparison.

Indeed, every aspect of St. Peter's is a bit outsized (just ask the Protestant reformers who railed against it). It took 176 years to complete (1450-1626), and its designers are a Renaissance all-star team. Donato Bramante, one of its first architects, handed the baton to Raphael, and it eventually ended up in the hands of Michelangelo. Along the way the shape of the church changed from a Greek cross, with four equal sides branching off a central dome, to a Latin cross, with a single, dominant long nave. But Bramante's great dome remains its centerpiece. Outside, Gianlorenzo Bernini's colonnaded entry plaza (1667), whose arms seem to open and welcome visitors in an embrace, is one of the world's finest arrival spaces.

To pray within these walls is to touch history. Here St. Peter was martyred. Here, after embracing Christianity, the Emperor Constantine first erected a basilica in the 4th century A.D. And here the Pope celebrates his church's most sacred annual observances. Here, present and past are as one. ∎

HANK WALKER—TIME LIFE PICTURES

PATRICIA CADLEY

CONCLAVE Summoned by Pope John XXIII, Cardinals gather in the long nave of St. Peter's on Oct. 11, 1962, to open the church's revolutionary council, Vatican II. The picture is more than 40 years old, but visitors to the church today would find little changed; in this space, time seems to hold its breath. At left is Bernini's entry plaza

WORSHIP

FAILLET—KEYSTONE—GAMMA

Sublime in its Simplicity

With the soaring swell of **Nôtre Dame du Haut,** architecture's stern master
of precision, Le Corbusier, created a building that breathes pure emotion

THE SWISS-BORN FRENCH ARCHITECT CHARLES-EDOUARD Jeanneret, who dubbed himself Le Corbusier, was an unlikely choice to design the Catholic church in the French village of Ronchamp: he was a lifelong atheist and socialist. Perhaps its historic sense of place inspired him: a destination for religious pilgrims since the 13th century, the hilltop was the site of a heroic last stand by French Resistance fighters in 1944, who were wiped out when German troops blew up the church in which they had taken refuge after a 10-week battle.

Le Corbusier began by ordering that the shards of the old church be collected—these broken stones would be worked into his design. Atop 10-ft.-thick walls that evoke a fortress, he placed a curved roof that seems to billow in the wind, evoking both the contours of a French nun's habit and the profile of a bird about to take flight. From the exterior, the building is a different shape on each side—while inside, small irregularly placed windows project onto the white walls a shifting, sliding drama of light and shadow. At Our Lady on High, the man who was one of Modernism's champions of the rational revealed his soul: in this space, geometry gives way to poetry, mathematical precision to intuitive lyricism, angular purity to a flowing surrealism. ■

Church of the Melting Spires

Antonio Gaudí began designing his masterpiece, **La Sagrada Familia**, in Barcelona in 1883. With luck, the cathedral will be complete by 2050

I N AN ERA WHEN INTELLECTUALS AND THEIR THEORIES dominated design, Antonio Gaudí was, above all, an architect of emotion. And the Gaudí project that aroused the greatest passions was the Templo Expiatori de la Sagrada Familia (Expiatory Church of the Holy Family), in his native Barcelona. Winning the commission in 1883 because one of the builders had dreamed he would hire an architect with blue eyes, Gaudi resolved to build Europe's tallest church, with a soaring Art Nouveau design. A Catholic zealot who once nearly succeeded in starving himself to death during a Lenten fast, Gaudí created a visionary—almost hallucinatory—structure. Its vertiginous towers seem to melt and swell like candles in the Spanish sun, while its encrusted layers of sculpture appear to sprout from the stone.

Nature eschews right angles, straight lines and perfect circles; thus Gaudí, as God's apprentice, did so too. Instead, he crafted a dizzying array of parabolas, hyperbolas, helices and helicoids—curving, open-ended forms that computer calculations would confirm, decades later, to be structurally perfect. More than a century in construction, Gaudí's masterpiece is now about half complete and is not expected to be finished until sometime near the middle of the 21st century. ∎

ANDREA JEMOLO—CORBIS

A Chrysalis for the Soul

When religion, architecture and Southern California intersect, the result is Philip Johnson's Crystal Cathedral, where the walls seem made of light

"LET THERE BE LIGHT" WERE THE WORDS WITH WHICH the God of the Old Testament began his great task of Creation. And ever since, when architects have set out to bring men closer to their maker, they have relied on light to evoke divine illumination: in the great cathedrals of the Middle Ages, the walls seem to disappear, overpowered by the radiance of enormous stained-glass windows. American architect Philip Johnson explored this idea even further with the spectacular church of glass he designed in Garden Grove, Calif., for the Protestant broadcasting evangelist Robert Schuller.

Schuller, a practitioner of muscular Christianity, got his start in 1955 by preaching outdoors to a flock gathered in their cars at a rented drive-in movie theater; by the 1970s he was preaching to a congregation of millions gathered around their TV sets on his weekly Sunday program *The Hour of Power.* A potent promoter of his vision, Schuller resolved in the late '70s to create a church that would capture the imagination, embody his theology of divinely inspired optimism—and make a suitably spectacular stu-

dio for his TV broadcasts. The preacher was also an architecture buff: he initially imagined that he could design the building himself. Disabused of this notion, he happened to read in TIME that Johnson was one of America's leading architects. That sold salesman Schuller, who gave Johnson a call.

Patron and architect were well matched: both like to make a splash. Johnson sketched out a star-shaped chamber that stretches 415 ft. on one axis and 207 ft. on the other. A marble pulpit fills one point of the star; balconies occupy the other three. Around and above this sanctuary, 128-ft. walls soar upward to meet a ceiling composed entirely of reflective glass. But it's the walls that draw the eye: their 10,900 tempered, silvered panels are held in place by a delicate lattice of 16,000 thin white steel trusses. The Crystal Cathedral might well be called the Chrysalis Cathedral: the effect is of being nestled in a great cocoon of light. But the structure's gossamer appearance is deceptive: it is designed to withstand 8.0 earthquakes and winds of 100 m.p.h.

When the building was completed in 1980, Schuller saw that it was good. "I remembered how wonderful it had been at my little drive-in church, where there had been no walls or ceiling," the televangelist recalled. "It was there I fell in love with the sky." ∎

CATHERINE KARNOW WOODFIN CAMP 2

HIGH LIGHT: The building seats 3,000 worshippers, who enter through a pair of 90-ft. glass doors. Robert Schuller was so delighted with his church-cum-broadcast-studio that 10 years after the Crystal Cathedral was completed, he asked architect Philip Johnson to design a bell tower for the complex. Johnson created a $5 million edifice (on the left in the main picture) made of polished stainless-steel prisms. At 234 ft., the campanile is so high it serves as a beacon for pilots seeking Orange County's nearby John Wayne Airport, south of Los Angeles

Where We Live

The essentials are a bouquet of gerunds: rooms for dining, sleeping, cooking, gathering. But when great designers seize this simple theme and ring changes on it, the results are often compelling. Because the assignment is so pared down, home design often seems the purest reflection of an architect's muse, from the classical pediments of Thomas Jefferson to the metal-mad modernism of Ludwig Mies van der Rohe or Pierre Koenig. Yes, we marvel at skyscrapers and concert halls, but when it comes to design, this is where the heart is

CASE STUDY HOUSE NO. 22 (STAHL HOUSE), LOS ANGELES
Pierre Koenig's 1960 masterpiece is cantilevered to highlight its best feature: a stunning view of L.A.

JULIUS SHULMAN PHOTOGRAPHY

In Sorrow's Wake, Preservation

Protected by a deep layer of volcanic ash after the eruption of Mount Vesuvius destroyed the city of Pompeii, the **House of the Vettii** offers a portal into the past

"YOU COULD HEAR THE SHRIEKS OF WOMEN, THE WAILING of infants, and the shouting of men," wrote Pliny the Younger, the most eloquent eyewitness to the explosion of Mount Vesuvius in the summer of A.D. 79. "Many … imagined there were no gods left, and that the universe was plunged into eternal darkness for evermore." But where Pliny found darkness, history has found light: the eruption of Vesuvius preserved the buildings of Pompeii, a Roman provincial capital, in a protective blanket of ash. Academics began to take serious interest in the ruins in the 1740s, thrilled to be able to walk into the homes of long-dead Romans.

The unearthing of Pompeii revealed in detail the vibrant lives of 1st century Romans and the buildings that housed them. The court-yard shown here is from the House of the Vettii, named for two brothers whose signet rings were found within it; they appear to have been former slaves who later prospered as wine merchants. The enclosed courtyard, which contained fountains and statues of marble and bronze, was designed to be visible from the street, the better to display the affluence of its upwardly mobile owners. The home's rounded arches, tiled roofs, colorful frescoes and colonnaded courtyard make up a template for domestic architecture in temperate climes; its echoes can be found in buildings ranging from Moorish Spain to medieval France to colonial Ecuador to modern-day Palm Springs. If Rome is the Eternal City, its architecture has proved an eternal influence. ∎

MIMMO JODICE-CORBIS; INSET: DAVE BARTRUFF-CORBIS

VANNI ARCHIVE-CORBIS. INSET: BETTMANN CORBIS

Fresh Life for Classical Forms

Poised between a dying Gothic era and a coming Age of Reason, Renaissance man Andrea Palladio found the future of design in its past at the serene **Villa Rotonda**

AN ARCHITECTURAL RIDDLE: WHAT COMMON SPIR- it underlies English castles, American pub- lic buildings, Swiss railroad stations, Spanish libraries, Tuscan villas and Canadian hotels? The answer: All these buildings echo the influence of the Greeks and Romans, as filtered through the genius of Renaissance man Andrea Palladio, the 16th century Italian architect whose reinterpretations of the design legacies of antiquity have been the dominant language of architec- ture for the past 400 years. The power, up- lift and simplicity of Palladio's work are best captured in Villa Rotonda, the country home he designed in the 1560s for Paolo Almerico, a retired cleric.

Crowning a hill in the Tuscan countryside, Villa Rotonda seems poised between heaven and earth. The gentle, graceful curve of its dome (inspired by the Pan- theon) reaches skyward, while the four identical porticoes that flank it anchor the house firmly to the ground. Its scale is just grand enough to in- spire but restrained enough not to overpow- er. Palladio rotated the corners of the house 45° away from the four points of the com- pass, so that each section would receive some sunlight throughout the day. Be- neath the dome, the central hall is adorned with pastel frescoes and gives way to square, severe rooms with high ceil- ings. A master of proportion, Palladio took the design vernacular of a pagan age—pedi- ments, porticoes and pillars, domes, arches and octagons—and gleaned from its clean Eu- clidean symmetries the blueprints for an Age of Reason. If you seek his monument, look around you.■

Fairy Tales and Nightmares

Repository of Czech culture for centuries, **Hradcany Castle** has emerged from a tortured period to once again embody its people's hopes and dreams

SLOW BUT SURE
Looming over the Vltava River, St. Vitus'
Cathedral is the highest point of the Hradcany
complex. It was begun in 1344
and completed in 1929

JOHN LAWRENCE—GETTY IMAGES

HRADCANY CASTLE, THE SOARING COMPLEX OF FORTI-fications, palaces, cathedrals and government offices that reigns over Prague's highest hilltop, is a glorious patchwork of different styles and eras, reflecting the 11 centuries over which it has been constructed. Bohemian princes lived and ruled here, as did Holy Roman Emperors. In 1618 two Bohemian noblemen were defenestrated here; the incident touched off the Thirty Years War. Foreign tyrants have also passed through: in World War II, Hradcany was the seat of S.S. General Reinhard Heydrich's murderous Nazi Occupation. In 1948 anticommunist leader Jan Masaryk fell to his death—or was defenestrated—from the Cernin Palace, and bureaucrats beholden to Moscow took power. And it was here that Czech students who dared to dream of freedom saw their ideals crushed by invading Soviet tanks in the Prague Spring of 1968.

Begun as a fort by Prince Boleslav in 973, when the Premyslid dynasty united the Czech nation for the first time, the walls of Hradcany were soon expanded to enclose a nearby cathedral built a generation earlier by King Wenceslas. By the time Charles IV, King of Bohemia, was crowned Holy Roman Emperor four centuries later, the complex had grown to include several more churches, a palace and a library. From Hradcany, Charles presided over a golden age in which Prague became the political and cultural center of the Continent. His successors added gates, gardens, towers and courtyards in a dizzying array of styles: Gothic, Baroque, Romanesque, Rococo. But instead of architectural chaos, this layering yielded a rich, somehow unified repository of Czech culture.

Hradcany has always resembled a fairy-tale castle; in recent decades, like a bewitched palace in a folk tale, it has finally awakened from decades of nightmares. General Heydrich was slain in 1942 by Czech patriots, and the Soviets were sent packing in 1990 after Czechoslovakia's "velvet revolution." Ironically, the first leader freely elected by Czechs in several generations, President Vaclav Havel, chose not to live in Hradcany. As a show of humility, this playwright turned politician used the castle as an office and reception center but lived in a small cottage not far from where a fellow writer and student of the absurd, Franz Kafka, once lived. ∎

ALL PHOTOS: © MONTICELLO / THOMAS JEFFERSON FOUNDATION INC.

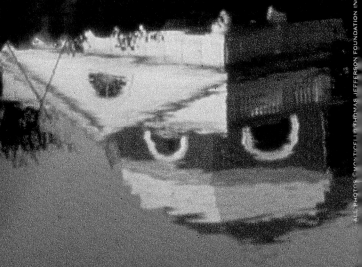

LIVE

A Study in Double Vision

Reflecting the genius who designed it, Thomas Jefferson's **Monticello** keeps one eye fixed on the past, while the other peers into the future

WHEN STILL IN HIS 20S, THOMAS JEFFERSON SCALED an 800-ft. mountain that his recently deceased father had willed to him and was transfixed by the majestic view it afforded of the Rivanna Valley below: "How sublime to look down into the workhouse of nature," he would later write, "to see her clouds, hail, snow, rain, thunder all fabricated at our feet!" He decided then and there he would build his home on this peak. Taking for its name an Italian phrase that translates loosely as "Little Mountain," he called it Monticello.

From the next six decades, Jefferson would not stop designing, building, demolishing and remodeling the home that he thought of as his life's work. "Architecture is my delight, and putting up and pulling down one of my favorite amusements," he admitted in his 50s. The result, Monticello, is as hard to pin

down as the genius who designed it: the man who worshiped liberty but held slaves; the radical egalitarian who was also a landed aristocrat; the thinker whose life was marked by a constant tension between idealism and practicality.

Jefferson's sense of balance resolved these opposing impulses into unified eloquence. On Monticello's West Portico, a montage of straight lines (triangles, rectangles and octagons) is arrayed beautifully against the gentle curves of stone pillars, balustrades, round windows and the fine dome, whose scale is exquisitely poised between the intimate and the grand, gently capping the hilltop. "I am as happy nowhere else," Jefferson once wrote, "and all my wishes end, where I hope my days will end, at Monticello." On July 4th, 1826—50 years to the day after the signing of the Declaration of Independence and within hours of the passing of his lifelong friend and rival, John Adams—Thomas Jefferson got his wish: he died in his bed at the home he had spent his life building. ∎

HAVING IT BOTH WAYS: Monticello's classical exterior and dome (the first in America) refer back to Greece and Rome via Palladio. But the interior is a fascinating amalgam of past and future. While the parlor and tearoom, above, are serenely classical, other elements of the interior were so modern as to seem bizarrely futuristic to 18th century eyes: a bed that was raised and lowered on pulleys, doors that were opened and closed by chains hidden beneath the floor and so on. Here the balance and serenity of the building's public face give way to an idiosyncratic riot—each of the 43 rooms is a unique size and shape. And the contradictions continue: the slaves who kept such grand homes functioning were housed in rudimentary quarters in a separate enclave on the grounds

Hearth of the Purloined Muse

Giving the slip to Victorian decorum, William Morris shaped the Arts and Crafts decorative style, built the lovely **Red House**—and didn't live happily ever after

WHEN ENGLISH DESIGNER WILLIAM MORRIS DECIDED to build a house for himself and his new bride in 1858, he asked his colleague, architect Philip Webb, to create a "joyful nook of heaven in an unheavenly world." Morris and Webb were founders of the English Arts and Crafts movement, which rebelled against stuffy Victorian homes that seemed designed, on the outside, to subdue nature and, on the inside, to regulate human conduct. So snugly is Red House nestled in Bexley Heath, Kent, that it appears to have grown there. Within, each room flows openly into the next, a stark departure from Victorian floor plans that sought to segregate their occupants by class, age and gender.

Morris' friend, the poet Dante Gabriel Rossetti, rhapsodized that the building was "more a poem than a house." He was similarly passionate about Morris' wife Janey, a muse and model for the artists, poets and painters who gathered at Red House. Within five years, Rossetti had stolen away his host's wife; Morris moved to London and never lived in Red House again. ■

DETAILS: Philip Webb added a minstrel's gallery to a settee in the vaulted drawing room; Morris designed the wallpaper

WALLPAPER, NTPL/JONATHAN GIBSON; DRAWING ROOM, NTPL/NADIA MACKENZIE

NTPL/ANDREW BUTLER

INSIDE Horta reserved most of his more elaborate Art Nouveau gestures for the interior of his home (now the Horta Museum), though there are a few ornamental railings on the façade, below. Few architects attempted to create exteriors in the new form; the Spaniard Antonio Gaudí was perhaps the most successful, but he had few disciples until long after his death

The New Angle: No Angles

Turning their backs on Euclid's geometries, architects of the Art Nouveau era reveled in the interplay of organic forms, as in Brussels' fine **Horta Museum**

DETERMINED TO CREATE AN ARCHITECTURE WHOSE roots were not in Greece and Rome—or in revivals of Gothic forms—architects of the late 19th century found their inspiration in the flowing shapes of nature. Declaring war on the right angle, they created buildings that seemed as if they had sprouted from the earth, rather than from a blueprint. Among the brightest lights of the movement were Antonio Gaudí in Spain, Charles Rennie Mackintosh in Scotland and Victor Horta in Belgium. Horta's town house in Brussels, which dates from 1898, is a model of the enormously popular new style, christened Art Nouveau. The house was restored and opened as the Horta Museum in 1969.

Inside, light from a great skylight washes through a central hall to bathe all the rooms in a soft glow. Banisters, mirrors, staircases and lamps extend tendrils of iron and brass; mirrors reflect the man-made garden into infinity. Alas, when Germany's stern modernists deemed ornamentation obsolete, Horta abandoned the style of his youth; for decades before his death in 1947, he designed neoclassical buildings. ■

RICHARD BRYANT—ARCAID.CO.UK (3)

Plutocrat's Pleasure Dome

Press lord William Randolph Hearst pursued an impossible dream: to create an estate big enough to house his ego. But his effort, **San Simeon,** is a hoot

CATHERINE KARNOW— WOODFIN CAMP (2)

A. RAMEY—WOODFIN CAMP (2)

FROM BOYHOOD, FUTURE MEDIA MOGUL WILLIAM RANdolph Hearst loved camping at the quarter-million-acre wilderness that his father, mining millionaire George Hearst, owned near San Simeon on the California coast, midway between Los Angeles and San Francisco. But the grown-up William decided that he preferred ceilings and beds to tents and sleeping bags. So he cabled his architect, Julia Morgan: "I would like to build a little something."

The problem: Hearst couldn't think little. After being kicked out of Harvard (for presenting his professors with chamber pots that had their names engraved inside), he took over a San Francisco newspaper his father had won gambling and parlayed it into a media empire that included newspapers, magazines, radio stations, a wire service and two film studios. Hearst's fortune and his imperial pretensions marched in lockstep. The first plan for La Cuesta Encantada (The Enchanted Hill) was for a few simple bungalows; these became three Italianate villas, which in turn became guest houses to an immense (60,000 sq. ft, 115 rooms) mansion, Casa Grande, based on a Spanish cathedral. Inside were thousands of paintings, statues, tapestries, carpets and antiques that Hearst's buyers had pillaged … uh … amassed from around the world.

An army of workers labored for more than 20 years in pursuit of Hearst's ever receding goal: to create an edifice as vast as his ego. During the Depression, it was the single largest nongovernment construction project in California. Work finally stopped in 1942, when Hearst was mired in debt. At his death in 1951, San Simeon remained unfinished. The Hearst family donated the estate to California in 1957; it remains unfinished to this day. Yes, it's a wild, clashing farrago of nostalgia, megalomania and random architectural styles, but it does achieve its purpose: it makes your jaw drop. ■

VERBATIM
"[Buildings] should charm by their detail rather than overwhelm by clumsy exuberance."
—Architect Julia Morgan, to W.R. Hearst

XANADU Filmmaker Orson Welles parodied San Simeon as "Xanadu" in his classic movie portrait of Hearst, *Citizen Kane.* A guest bedroom and baronial library, top, seem sized for giants, not men. The classical swimming pool, which includes 17 century Italian bas-reliefs, was demolished and rebuilt three times before Heart was satisfied with it. San Simeon's grounds once included five greenhouses, the world's largest private zoo and an airport

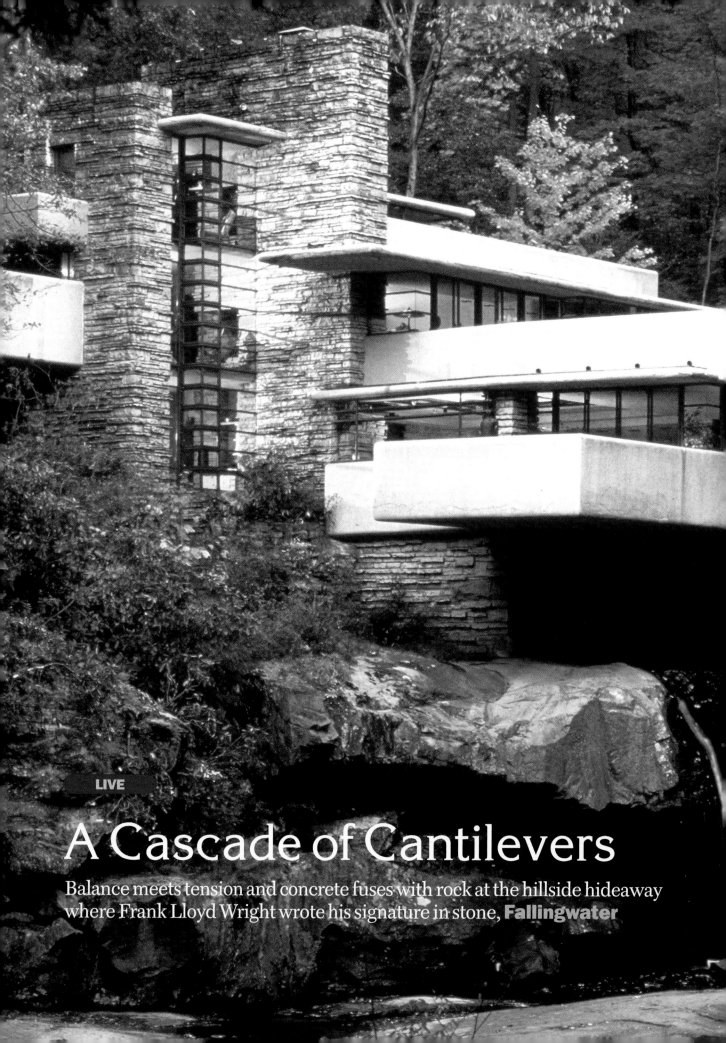

A Cascade of Cantilevers

Balance meets tension and concrete fuses with rock at the hillside hideaway where Frank Lloyd Wright wrote his signature in stone, **Fallingwater**

CHRISTOPHER LITTLE—CORBIS

EZRA STOLLER—ESTO

HARMONY: Wright marries the cozy and the capacious in the home's serene, inviting interior. Said University of Pittsburgh architectural historian Franklin Toker in his engrossing study of the building of the house, *Fallingwater Rising* (Knopf; 2003): The house's spell "has only a little to do with architecture and engineering: the quality we perceive here is essentially spiritual … It is not the modernity but the antiquity—even the eternality—of Fallingwater that enthralls us"

THE MOST FAMOUS—AND, ARGUABLY, THE MOST BEAUTI-ful—house built in the 20th century is a fusion of rock, water and concrete, of nature's undulating lines and the architect's geometrical planes, where the handiwork of geology and man are melded in easy, eternal balance. To behold Fallingwater, a house that is a seamless part of the cascading creek it is perched above, is to realize how each completes the other. Seeing is believing: this is what Frank Lloyd Wright meant by "organic" architecture.

In the mid-1930s, just as Wright's career was scraping bottom, he was hired by Pittsburgh department-store impresario Edgar J. Kaufman, whose son had once studied with Wright, to design a weekend retreat at his dairy farm in the Pennsylvania countryside. Both Kaufman (who had been snubbed by Pittsburgh society because he was Jewish) and Wright (whose work had fallen out of fashion with the ascendancy of Mies van der Rohe's International Style) were eager to create a landmark that would bring them the respect they craved.

The result, well, made a splash. Hailed by journalists eager to champion American architecture, Fallingwater swiftly rose to worldwide renown upon its completion in 1939. But it's more than hype that makes people love this building: Fallingwater is Wright's masterpiece. From the outside, it hovers weightlessly over the waterfall. Within, Wright evokes the feel of the surrounding forest, with rooms that open like clearings, windows that pull outdoor spaces inside, and outcroppings of natural rock that bind building and site.

As usual, Wright's design is least perfect where least visible. The architect was, at best, indifferent about engineering, and Kaufman spent the rest of his life worrying that not enough structural steel had been used in the heavy, cantilevered concrete terraces, which began to crack even before the structure was completed—though Wright's apprentices, without the master's knowledge, had specified twice as much steel as he had called for. Sure enough, in the 1990s engineers declared that the building was about to fall into the creek (and might have decades earlier, but for the extra steel), and Fallingwater underwent an emergency, $11 million makeover. But this building's glories more than make up for its engineering flaws. Wright spent decades proclaiming he was a genius; Fallingwater argues his case better, without saying a word. ∎

GEORGE LAMBROS

Making It Perfectly Clear

In Ludwig Mies van der Rohe's elegant exercise in transparency and
restraint outside Chicago, **Farnsworth House,** the reign is of the plain

VERBATIM
"[It] has become less a device for living and more a device for making people think about the ways we choose to live"
—Verlyn Klinkenborg

AFTER A SHOWER, EDITH FARNSWORTH STEPPED OUT of her bathroom—the only enclosed, private space in the open-plan glass house her friend Ludwig Mies van der Rohe had designed for her—and was confronted by a gaggle of Japanese tourists standing outside her transparent walls, snapping pictures. Such are the pitfalls of living in a Miesian masterpiece. Consisting of sheer glass walls hung between two horizontal planes of marble, the Farnsworth House (1951) is suspended 5 ft. above the Illinois soil by eight evenly spaced steel columns that evoke the elegant symmetry of a Greek temple. At night it is a floating rectangle of light, hovering over the grass—a breathtaking effect that Mies refused to spoil by adding curtains to his windows.

Farnsworth had greater problems than nosy sightseers. The glass walls make the home a hothouse in summer: only one window opens, and Mies didn't want air-conditioning machinery ruining his sleek lines. In winter, the poorly insulated building freezes and the windows fog up. In spring, when the nearby Fox River spills over its banks, the house is accessible only by canoe. In 1972, the frustrated Farnsworth sold the 2,000-sq.-ft. house to British builder (and Mies acolyte) Lord Peter Palumbo, who painstakingly restored and preserved it. In 2003, this platonic ideal of a domicile was forever relieved of the need to accommodate the mundane concerns of human beings: Palumbo sold it to the National Trust for Historic Preservation, and it will become a museum. ∎

Giddy Grid for a Casual Culture

As Americans left the cities for the suburbs, they craved a new, less formal style of living. California had the answer in the laid-back flair of the **Eames House**

WORLD WAR II WAS WON AND A GENERATION OF YOUNG soldiers was returning home. So John Entenza, the owner and editor of *Arts & Architecture* magazine, commissioned a series of 24 new houses in the Los Angeles area to explore how to put roofs over the heads of millions of young families. Several ideas pioneered in these "Case Studies," such as the use of sliding glass doors to fuse indoor and outdoor space and the reversal of the traditional floor plan by placing the living room at the back of the home, away from the street, became standard features of 1950s housing. The home that best suited the era's emerg-

ing lifestyles was Case Study No. 8, by husband and wife designers Charles and Ray Eames.

For their Pacific Palisades home and workspace, the duo worked entirely from parts available at any building supply vendor: standard 4-in., H-shaped columns; factory windows with X-trusses between them. They jazzed up this utilitarian façade with color panels in a geometric grid that recalls the paintings of Piet Mondrian. Inside, Case Study No. 8 has few walls, allowing for a maximum of flexibility and spaciousness, and a spiral staircase from a marine supply catalog. "If you are really going to involve people," Charles Eames said, "you must open the door in an intriguing and fascinating way." Case Study No. 8 opened the doors of a million knock-offs. ∎

JULIUS SHULMAN (2)

EZRA STOLLER—ESTO (2)

Out of the Woods

Finnish architect Alvar Aalto brought the forest indoors at his flowing, shade-dappled retreat, the **Villa Mairea**

HE IS A GENIUS," FRANK LLOYD WRIGHT SAID AFTER SEE-ing the work that brought Alvar Aalto fame in America, the Finnish Pavilion at the 1939 World's Fair in New York. Like Wright, the Finn tried to meld modernism's hard, technological edges with the softer, organic forms of nature. And as with Wright, one of Aalto's masterpieces is a small private country home, built for wealthy friends.

In 1937, Harry and Maire Gullichsen, who ranked among Finland's leading industrialists, commissioned Aalto to build a retreat for them in a pine forest near the town of Noormarkku. They asked for a home that was both modern and Finnish, both elegant and unostentatious, both rustic and progressive. To square each of these circles, Aalto turned to collage, with its ability to weave disparate, clashing elements into a single cohesive whole. He created a patchwork home that stitched together traces of Finnish farm architecture, Gothic churches and influences from as far afield as California and Japan. But a single theme resonates most: pine logs, wooden poles and steel posts covered in rattan or birch appear throughout Villa Mairea, evoking its forest setting, and the larger culture and landscape of Finland. Like Fallingwater's, Villa Mairea's floor plan is a series of flowing internal spaces that mimics branching forest paths. As a result, this intriguing architectural experiment is also a supremely livable space. ∎

Twelve Houses, River View

Composite dwellings have seldom attracted great designers—but there are a few fine buildings that unite many residential units into a delightful whole

GROUCHO MARX MIGHT HAVE BEEN THINKING OF THE picture at right when he uttered his famous challenge after being caught in a compromising position: "Who are you going to believe? Me—or your own lying eyes?" In this case, your own lying eyes are looking at a striking apartment building that has not yet been built: it only exists as a composite digital image on the computers at the firm of architect Santiago Calatrava. The picture depicts the building as it may appear—if and when it is ever built—at a site in lower Manhattan, near the South Street Seaport along the East River, offering views of both the Statue of Liberty and the Brooklyn Bridge.

Calatrava's design calls for 12 cube-shaped largely glass town houses, 45 ft. on each side, that will be attached to a central vertical core containing elevators, stairways, plumbing and electric lines. The building would top out at 835 ft.; its eight-story base is intended to house a museum or restaurant. The individual cubes, which cantilever off the structure, would be lifted into position and suspended one at a time from the central core, which serves as a kind of vertical truss. Designed for the wealthiest of clients, each of these luxury "town houses in the sky" is intended for the use of only one or two families, and will have its own internal elevators as well as space for a garden and terrace on the roof. The price for each unit will likely be in the tens of millions of dollars.

Well, that's the plan, according to developer Frank Sciame. Will the building begin to rise in 2006, as Sciame fervently hopes? It's far too soon to tell; such plans are always, well, up in the air. The good news is that Calatrava's design is only one of several new proposals for apartment buildings in New York City that are stimulating hopes for a worldwide renaissance in designs for multifamily structures: Frank Gehry and Norman Foster have also announced plans to create eye-catching new apartment buildings in New York City.

The history of the apartment building only rarely crosses paths with the history of great design. The cliff dwellings of the Pueblo Indians, while fascinating, are of interest more to the anthropologist than the architect. Apartment buildings generally favor function over style, and city town houses—with the notable exception of the Royal Crescent in Bath, Britain, and a few other adventurous examples—are generally just mansions shorn of their sides, stuffed together and extruded skyward, to make up in height what they lack in width. Calatrava's proposed building shares some qualities with the most notable attempt to bring fresh vision to apartment buildings: Moshe Safdie's Habitat complex, built for the Expo 67 World's Fair in Montreal. Safdie hoped to create a new paradigm for construction in which individual concrete units could be prefabricated, brought to a site and assembled, allowing for both efficiency and versatility. The result, Habitat, is a fascinating building, but it failed to start a revolution. ■

SANTIAGO CALATRAVA S.A.—©DAVID SUNDBERG—ESTO

Casa Milá

Pueblo Dwelling

TOP: ROBERT FRERCK—WOODFIN CAMP; BOTTOM: TOM BEAN—CORBIS

CASA MILÁ, BARCELONA, 1910 Antonio Gaudí's building undulates its way around a right-angled city corner, resembling a concoction sculpted out of whipped cream. The building is also known as the Stone Quarry; behind its façade, the apartments form a circle around a central courtyard. Gaudí's unique, flowing forms strongly influenced the work of Eero Saarinen and Santiago Calatrava

PUEBLO INDIAN DWELLING These descendants of the Anasazi Indians live in desert regions of the American Southwest in large adobe communes, which are terraced. Upper floors are reached by a system of trapdoors and ladders. The difficult access is a safety measure designed to slow an enemy's penetration of the complex

Habitat

HABITAT, MONTREAL, 1967
Canadian-Israeli architect Moshe Safdie designed a futuristic building that consists of 354 individual precast concrete units connected by internal steel cables. The complex includes 158 separate apartments, which range in size from one room to five or six. Every apartment has a terrace, and many have gardens

ROYAL CRESCENT, BATH, U.K., 1767
With real estate in cities so precious, the attached town house is a staple of upper-class urban living. The Royal Crescent in Bath, which connects distinct units in a sweeping semi-circle around a city park, is a notable success in bringing life to the form. Architect John Wood and his father helped introduce the concept of urban planning to Britain and the world

Royal Crescent

TOP: LEE SNIDER—CORBIS. BOTTOM: LONDON AERIAL PHOTO LIBRARY—CORBIS

The Great Iconoclast

His outsize persona may have been his greatest creation, but beneath the bombast, Frank Lloyd Wright was the genius he claimed to be

LIKE HIS FAMED GUGGENHEIM MUSEUM—A LONE, defiant circle thumbing its nose at Manhattan's relentless right-angle grid—Frank Lloyd Wright wasn't made to fit in. He never earned a degree in architecture. He built only a handful of skyscrapers, the buildings with which many 20th century designers made their reputations. And almost alone among recent major architects, he hated cities, believing that mankind's utopian future lay in agrarian communes where structures and nature would be one.

Wright was a dyspeptic smart-aleck who referred to the International Style pioneered by his rival, Ludwig Mies van der Rohe, as "neither international nor a style" and challenged wealthy clients by ranting about "unnatural reservoirs of

predatory capital." He was always itching to found a bona fide "movement"—Prairie Style, Organic Style, Usonian Style and so on—and his various autobiographies read more like manifestos than memoirs. He was vain, a crank in a purple cape who habitually lied about his age and often behaved like an aspiring cult leader—gathering around him small armies of acolytes to live communally at rustic compounds in Wisconsin and Arizona.

Yet Wright was far from a poseur: he invented a new, uniquely American aesthetic that owed nothing to inherited European forms. Asked to name other architects who had influenced him, he replied, with his usual modesty, "None."

Reading Emerson and Thoreau from an early age, Wright grew up believing that one man's vision of truth could reshape the world. In his early 20s, he set out to do just that, with (as he put it) "a hod of mortar and some bricks." Born in 1867, he apprenticed under the great Chicago architect Louis Sullivan (to whose famous dictum, "Form follows function," Wright rejoined, "Form and function are one"). Wright established an early reputation building private homes in the suburbs of Chicago that were unlike any residences seen before.

From the outside, these houses were unusual, in a surprisingly unobstrusive way. Where boxlike, two- or three-story Victorian homes dominated their settings, Wright's long, low houses, all horizontal planes, blended harmoniously with their surroundings. "No house should ever be on a hill or on anything," he would say later. "It should be of the hill, belonging to it." It was the interiors of these homes that were radically different: indoor rooms flowed seamlessly into outdoor spaces; tiny hallways opened onto vast, expansive chambers; natural light flowed from one part of the building to another throughout the day. From the first, Wright displayed an almost magical ability to manipulate space: stretching and compressing it, molding and bending it to his will.

Wright's Prairie Style homes brought fame and success, and he began seeking out larger projects. He devoted himself to his working retreat in the Wisconsin countryside, where he had spent summers as a child. Called Taliesin (Welsh for "shining brow"), this 600-acre pastoral enclave became Wright's home, studio, architecture school and farm. Here he gathered family, students and admirers to live as a self-sustaining community, in strict conformance with Wright's ideas about, well, pretty much everything: the fields were planted to yield crops based on the master's approved color scheme.

In 1916 Wright was awarded his first truly monumental commission, the Imperial Hotel in Tokyo. He devised an ingenious system of structural supports that kept the hotel intact during a devastating 1923 earthquake that flattened almost all the buildings around it. The structure could not withstand the pressure of commercial redevelopment, however; it was demolished in 1968.

Tremors also rocked Wright's personal life. In 1909 he left his wife and children to take up with the wife of a client; she was in turn murdered (along with her two children and four of Wright's associates) by a disgruntled servant at Taliesin, who then burned the place to the ground. Taliesin was rebuilt, but bankruptcy, depression and ever shifting professional fortunes would plague Wright for the rest of his life.

The 1930s brought more Wright masterpieces, including Fallingwater, a private home in Pennsylvania, and the Johnson Wax headquarters in Racine, Wis., which LIFE magazine in 1938 compared to "a woman swimming naked in a stream … cool, gliding, musical in movement and manner." He also

WERNER BISCHOF—MAGNUM PHOTOS. INSET: TALIESIN EAST INTERIOR WINDOW: FARRELL GREHAN—CORBIS

VERBATIM
"The physician can bury his mistakes, but the architect can only advise his clients to plant vines."
—Frank Lloyd Wright

designed a second communal retreat, Taliesin West in Arizona, where he spent much of the rest of his life.

By the 1940s, Wright had become a folk hero to those disaffected with the International Style and its theory that buildings should be "machines for living." Novelist Ayn Rand loosely based *The Fountainhead*, her celebration of individualism, on Wright's vision of architecture. (Wright, true to form, did everything he could to alienate the admiring Rand.) After World War II, Wright developed the Usonian Style (named, depending on whom you believe, for the word *us* or the abbreviation for United States), hoping to build attractive, inexpensive homes for middle-class Americans. But he was no master of utility. The roofs of his buildings leaked more often

than not, his creations were notoriously difficult (and expensive) to heat, and he regularly poured scalding contempt on clients who requested even minor changes in his designs.

A control freak, he would visit homes he had designed and argue with the owners over where the furniture (which he also usually designed) should be placed. He even attempted to style clothing for clients to wear in his buildings: no sale. When he died in 1959 (at 89), Wright—as he no doubt would have preferred—was both hailed and dismissed. In the years before his death, when Wright was struggling to find work, rival Philip Johnson snidely termed him "the best American architect of the 19th century." Maybe so—but it's telling that even Johnson's put-down includes an encomium. ∎

Robie House

Robie House

Taliesin West

Taliesin East

ROBIE HOUSE, OAK PARK, ILLINOIS, 1909 The residence's cantilevered roofs carefully shield it from the street and disguise the enormous banks of windows that bring natural light into the home. Once inside, visitors find the rather imposing exterior gives way to a sense of spaciousness and modern, streamlined glamour, created by the high ceilings, extensive windows and richly detailed woodwork. In the home's private rooms, the ceilings are quite low—Wright called the feel "democratic," but critics contend he was designing to fit his own rather diminutive (5 ft. 7 in.) size. The home's strong horizontal lines issue from Wright's conviction that a building should merge with its setting—in this case the flat landscape of the American Midwest. The building is now owned by the University of Chicago and is a National Historic Landmark.

TALIESIN WEST, ARIZONA, 1937 As with the Robie House, which he designed decades before, Wright hid the windows beneath the roofline in this desert workshop, which is flooded with natural light in the daytime. Wright's students helped build the structure, pouring concrete over native stone placed in forms to create the walls. Redwood columns support the roof.

TALIESIN EAST, WISCONSIN, 1925 Wright's interiors were made to order. He generally designed every element of the home: lights, chairs and desks, rug patterns and the colored insets in the windows. The joined windows at left open up the view, while disguising the corner of the house. Wright preferred to work with local stone, which he often left unfinished, as he sought to achieve an organic unity between site and structure.

❝ I [had] to choose between honest arrogance and a hypocritical

Imperial Hotel

Johnson Wax Building

Johnson Wax Building

IMPERIAL HOTEL, TOKYO, 1916-22
Wright's masterwork was demolished in 1968. Of its Asian feel, he wrote, "I have sometimes been asked why I did not make the opus more 'modern' ... there was a tradition there worthy of respect and I felt it my duty as well as my privilege to make the building belong to them so far as I might."

JOHNSON WAX BUILDING, 1936-39
The interior is a soaring, ennobling temple of commerce, a far cry from the cramped quarters allotted to most office workers. Opaque windows allow light to enter but don't offer workers a view outside. Wright designed three-legged chairs that tip over if the worker's posture isn't correct.

JOHNSON WAX BUILDING GARAGE Wright echoed the lily-pad shapes of the building's interior columns in the underground car park, where the streamlined curves of a late-'30s roadster look completely at home. The architect's early Prairie Style was angular, featuring long horizontal planes and severe right angles. Later in his career, Wright began to explore more fluid and fanciful forms, experiments that would culminate in the delicious spiral of New York City's Guggenheim Museum.

ROBIE HOUSE EXTERIOR: TIME PIX INC.—TIME LIFE PICTURES; ROBIE HOUSE INTERIOR: THOMAS A. HEINZ—CORBIS; TALIESIN WEST: CATHERINE KARNOW—WOODFIN CAMP; TALIESIN EAST INTERIOR WINDOW: FARRELL GREHAN—CORBIS; IMPERIAL HOTEL: HULTON ARCHIVE; JOHNSON WAX INTERIOR OF OFFICE: EZRA STOLLER—ESTO; JOHNSON WAX GARAGE: TORKEL KORLING—TIME LIFE PICTURES

humility ... the world knows what I chose. " —Frank Lloyd Wright

Where the
Arts Live

Daring architecture demands daring patrons. Popes and princes played the part in centuries past, but today's underwriters of great design are more likely to be unremarkable board members of arts institutions in search of a remarkable face for their museum or library—eye candy to put them on the cultural map. And when these modern-day Medicis meet a form-giver of genius … well, had you ever heard of Bilbao before 1997?

TIBOR BOGNAR—CORBIS

GUGGENHEIM MUSEUM, BILBAO, SPAIN
Frank Gehry's titanium-clad marvel (1997) has attracted millions of visitors to a once-obscure city

SESTINI AGENCY—GAMMA

Mother Ship of Music Halls

Birthplace of the operas of Donizetti, Rossini and Verdi, **Teatro Alla Scala** was destroyed in World War II, but rose from the ashes to raise its voice again

OPERA LOVERS THE WORLD OVER, NO MATTER WHICH flag they were born under, call one place their spiritual home: Milan's Teatro Alla Scala, better known by its abbreviated name, La Scala. When the city's previous opera house, the Regio Ducal Teatro, burned down in the 1770s, the Austrian Empress Maria Theresa, who then ruled Milan, commissioned architect Giuseppe Piermarini to design a replacement. The Empress underwrote the project by deeding the plot on which it would stand to local nobles who coveted private boxes in the theater, and then charging them a membership fee.

Piermarini designed a façade (it took five versions before his work suited the over-the-top tastes of his patrons) featuring neoclassical arches and a pediment that depicts Apollo racing in his chariot. But it is the interior of La Scala that truly sings; it seems cozy and familiar, though it seats 1,800. Yet it is grand, as well: its horseshoe of six tiers of box seats surrounds the two-level Royal Box, which perches over the entrance to the theater, directly opposite the stage, and draws the visitor's attention like a second, miniature proscenium.

An honor roll of great Italian composers—Donizetti, Bellini, Rossini and Verdi—has written for this stage. It was here that Verdi staged his first opera, *Oberto*, in 1839; he returned later in life, after a feud with management that kept him away for more than 20 years, to premiere his last masterpieces, *Otello* in 1887 and *Falstaff* in 1893.

JOHN HESELTINE—CORBIS

OUTSIDE: Architect Giuseppe Piermarini's eighteenth-century neoclassical façade was rebuilt in 1945

For much of the 20th century, La Scala remained the private property of the titled families who owned its boxes, which were decorated with their heraldic coats of arms and passed down from one generation to the next. The theater was flattened by an Allied bombing raid in World War II, but the Milanese so cherish La Scala that once the war ended they chose to rebuild it before any other structure in the city, even ahead of desperately needed housing and hospital facilities. Now owned by a foundation, the theater was closed for a controversial interior remodeling in 2002 (management swears it will be faithful to Piermarini's original design, but local preservationists are skeptical). It is scheduled to reopen with a gala performance in December 2004. ■

NIK WHEELER—CORBIS

The Royal Albert Hall is Britain's "village hall": within its elliptical walls, Olympic athletes contended, Winston Churchill spoke, Sir Laurence Olivier performed Shakespeare, the Beatles sang, and J.K. Rowling read *Harry Potter* books to children. Despite its imperfect acoustics and feeble ventilation system (both of which were greatly improved by a 10-year renovation completed in 2004), the Albert ranks in the affections of Britons somewhere between Big Ben and Benny Hill.

The hall is the brainchild of Prince Albert, Queen Victoria's royal consort, who dreamed of creating what some detractors called "Albertropolis"—a cultural, scientific and academic city within a city that would continue to attract the international intelligentsia who had flocked to the great London Exhibition of 1851.

Using profits from the exhibition, Albert purchased an estate in Kensington, not far from the site of the famed Crystal Palace, and set about erecting his Xanadu, which he envisioned as grand performance and exhibition spaces that would seat 30,000 spectators. He enlisted Henry Cole, who had assisted the Prince on several public works projects, as his architect. Before the first stone could be laid, however, Albert died of typhoid fever in 1861. When the hall opened in 1871, its name was changed to honor its founder. Funding woes reduced its size from Albert's grandiose plans; it still seats 7,000 listeners — very large for a concert hall.

In the decades after the auditorium opened, the campus of cultural ferment that Albert envisioned blossomed all around it: the area is now home to the Imperial College of Science, Technology, and Medicine; the Royal College of Art; the Victoria and Albert Museum; the Science Museum; the Natural History Museum; and the Royal Geographical Society. So it's fitting that the Royal Albert Hall is crowned by an 800-ft. frieze that circles the building and is inscribed with these words: "This Hall was erected for the advancement of the Arts and Sciences and works of industry of all nations in fulfillment of the intention of Albert, Prince Consort."

Triangular Triumph

Uniting ancient forms, modern materials and a revered site, I.M. Pei's glass pyramid re-energized the **Louvre Museum**

THE LOUVRE MUSEUM IS A LIVING repository of French history. Long the Paris palace of France's kings, it bears the fingerprints of medieval monarchs, Renaissance architects, 17th century sculptors and the Emperors Napoleon I and III. Routinely described as the world's foremost museum, it is the home of the Winged Victory of Samothrace, the Venus de Milo and the Mona Lisa. But since 1989 the Louvre's art and history have played second fiddle to its geometry: people can't stop talking about the pyramid.

In the early 1980s, French President François Mitterrand asked the Sino-American architect I.M. Pei to reinvent the Louvre to accommodate the millions of visitors it attracts each year. Pei's visionary proposal: placing a huge glass pyramid smack in the middle of the historic edifice's central courtyard. Its translucent triangles would serve as an entry portal, funneling visitors (and natural light) underground into a modern entrance complex.

When Pei's plans were unveiled in 1984, Parisians reviled the pyramid. Here, they charged, was a slice of Modernism dropped with no concern for context into a hallowed site. Mitterrand was branded "Mitterramses." And as for Pei: Well, why not revive the guillotine?

But—*sacre bleu!*—the big glass mass works. Its formal shape is of a piece with the French capital's neoclassical buildings and classical gardens. It offers visitors a memorable, efficient welcome. But the pyramid's true greatness lies in the sheer audacity of its conception. Eschewing the safe path of concealing a modern building within a shell designed to ape its surroundings, Pei argues with this startling juxtaposition that modern buildings can take their place alongside the finest of the past, if they offer a vision that is grand enough—and clear enough. ■

STEPHEN SIMPSON—TAXI—GETTY IMAGES

INSIDE STORY Under the courtyard level, the glass structure is revealed to be a double pyramid, whose lower portion channels sunlight into a central reception area that includes shops, cafés and other services. Architect Pei says the pyramid was inspired by the work of the master gardener Andre Le Notre, whose layout of the formal gardens at Versailles features strong geometric elements. The pyramid, 71 ft. high and 116 ft. on each side, is well placed within the larger street grid of Paris, aligning the museum with the Arc de Triomphe and the Place de la Concorde

MARVIN E. NEWMAN—WOODFIN CAMP

HISTORY
The site of a fortress and palace in the Middle Ages, the Louvre as we know it was begun under King François I in 1546. The architect was Pierre Lescot

Shock Treatment

A high-tech Tinkertoy, the **Pompidou Centre** in Paris invites us to view the museum as a fun house

ART AND PARIS? THE TWO BELONG TOGETHER, LIKE Hemingway and an apértif. But if art lovers the world over think of Paris as their spiritual home, Parisians were skeptical in 1968, when London and New York City were all the rage, and rioting students took to the streets of the Left Bank to denounce their nation's culture and politics. In 1969 the French government decided to build a new center of art, music and learning that would re-establish Paris as a cultural mecca. The competition to design this center (which would eventually bear the name of French President Georges Pompidou) attracted the short list of that

era's architectural superstars. So the design world was astounded when the plan of two young unknowns, Italian Renzo Piano and Briton Richard Rogers, was selected.

Their building was as radical as the rhetoric that inspired it: a playful cacophony of periscope-style ducts and air vents, it looms against the Paris sky as if still under construction, while a tubular Plexiglas caterpillar of an escalator zigzags up its façade. Splashed in bright, primary colors, it resembles a comic-book drawing of a factory. The Pompidou Centre put its novel style—high tech—on the map. In part an insolent slap in the face of the Establishment that funded it, this

DEREK CROUCHER—CORBIS

YANN ARTHUS-BERTRAND—CORBIS

WHEE! Amid the gray-brown streets of Paris, the Pompidou Centre's façade of primary colors stands out like a Lego block tossed in a mud puddle. The building doesn't just expose such usually hidden service elements as heating ducts and supporting girders; it delights in them. Toying with the notions of what we expect from a museum, the structure is an early example of architecture as Pop Art

museum-as-playhouse also argued that fine art didn't have to take itself seriously. Moreover, all were welcome here: the giddy escalator ride, with its great views of Paris, was free.

After its 1977 opening, the Pompidou Centre quickly became the toast of Paris, drawing five times as many visitors each year as its builders had anticipated. Indeed, heavy traffic necessitated a $120 million overhaul in 1997, during which the admission booth was moved to the foot of the escalator: the views of Paris are now reserved for paying customers. Like the students of 1968, in middle age the Pompidou Centre has succumbed to the blandishments of success. ■

A CRITIC
Standing outside the building one day, Richard Rogers told an elderly woman he was its architect. The response: "She hit me with her umbrella"

Art's Shining City on a Hill

When architect Richard Meier won the commission to design the immense **Getty Center** in Los Angeles, he rose to the occasion—and now, so do we

ART AL FRESCO: The temperate Los Angeles climate allowed Meier to create outdoor "rooms" at the complex, as visitors move along colonnades and plazas between buildings. With a vast site and multiple elevations to work with, Meier's design offers surprising vistas, hidden nooks and unexpected changes in height. A large, mazelike garden by noted landscape designer Robert Irwin anchors the bottom of the site, whose exterior spaces are surprisingly free of art—perhaps because architecture is the star of this particular L.A. story

FOUNTAIN: ROBERT LANDAU-CORBIS; COLONNADE: ART SEITZ/GAMMA

WHEN *TIME* REPORTED THE NEWS THAT THE MODernist American architect Richard Meier had been chosen to design the new J. Paul Getty Center in Los Angeles, Ronald Reagan was President, and Britney Spears was three years old: remember 1984? It would be seven years before the plans for Meier's complex of six separate buildings were finally unveiled, and another six years before the $1 billion museum finally opened on its sublime setting, a hilltop above west Los Angeles. The lofty 110-acre site, which offers sweeping views of L.A., works in tandem with Meier's severely handsome cluster of buildings to evoke constant comparisons to another brilliant merging of nature's work with man's: this is indeed an American Acropolis. And why stop there? As ar-

chitecture critic Reyner Banham declared at the time, "Not since the Roman emperors built their summer villas on the isle of Capri has there been an opportunity like this."

The Getty Center pays tribute to the ancients in its ethos as well. The millions of visitors it attracts park their cars at the base of the hill and ascend to the museum aboard a sleek monorail. The inescapable message: art is something above and beyond our mundane concerns, nobly elevated to a higher plane. In an era when many museums are actively seeking closer involvement with patrons' everyday lives, the Getty Center remains proudly aloof on its pedestal.

But there is no equivocating about the quality of Meier's buildings. Working assuredly on a vast canvas, the disciple of Le Corbusier and Mies van der Rohe designed a complex in which strong Euclidean forms—domes, sweeping curves, half-circles—are executed in gleaming, creamy modern materials and Italian travertine. The individual components sometimes appear to be abstract collages; with only dark windows and steel stair rails for exterior ornament, they are quite reserved. But their reticence is apt, for with a clutch of buildings and a striking site, this lily doesn't need much gilding. Said Meier before the first stone was laid: "The relationship of landscape to architecture, of interior to exterior, of climate to the building, is something that will be quite wonderful"—a promise an ancient designer of imperial villas on Capri might have made. Meier kept his promise, memorably. ∎

JOSEPH SOHM-CHROMOSOHM INC.-CORBIS

DOUGLAS SLONE-CORBIS

Visions of a Void

Daniel Libeskind found a design language that let him speak of the unspeakable in his jarring, moving **Jewish Museum of Berlin**

FOR ALMOST TWO DECADES, DANIEL LIBESKIND WAS THE world's most respected virtual architect: though he had been an influential critic, writer, teacher and theorist since the early 1980s, he had never actually built anything. The project that drew him from the comfort of a podium to the turmoil of a building site was the Jewish Museum of Berlin. Eighty-five members of the Jewish architect's family were murdered by the Nazis, and his father barely survived a German concentration camp.

In 1988, when the city from which Hitler had orchestrated the Final Solution opened a competition to design a museum of Jewish history, Libeskind entered the fray. In announcing his design had won (and admitting that it was deeply uncon-

ventional), the jury noted that "the obvious thing may have been to build a normal museum, had not one entry put forward a quite extraordinary, profound response."

When the museum opened in 2001, "extraordinary" and "profound" seemed understated. Outside, the building is a dissonant, zigzagging jumble of polygons wrapped in titanium and zinc. The shape may seem arbitrary, but its outline evokes the jagged shards of a shattered Star of David, a bolt of lightning, or even the letter *S* as it appeared on the uniforms of Hitler's SS troops. Inside, three walkways trace the three paths taken by Germany's Jews under Nazi rule—exile, death or (for a fortunate few) survival—and offer a chance to follow the story told in the museum. One path leads to a Garden of

STABBED: Inside, windows slash through the walls at odd angles, like knife wounds. What seems random is not: Libeskind obtained from the German government a list of all the Berlin Jews who died in the Holocaust. He plotted their addresses on a map of the city and then drew lines to the places beyond the city limits where they were murdered or found refuge. These lines fixed the placement and angle of the windows, one of which points directly to Auschwitz. At right are the fifth and final void, within the building, and the jagged windows, seen from the outside

Exile, whose 48 stone columns represent the year of Israel's founding, 1948); another leads to the Holocaust Tower, which resembles a chimney; the last leads to the Stairs of Continuity, which bring visitors to the main exhibition space.

A series of empty spaces puncture the walls, floors and ceilings throughout the museum. Libeskind calls these dimly lighted, raw concrete abscesses, in which no exhibits will be housed, voids. They serve as silent, eloquent reminders that this museum, which enshrines the culture and history of Germany's Jews, is, more than anything else, about the culture that is not there, because it was wiped out; about the history that is not there, because it was erased; and about the people who are not there, because they were annihilated. ∎

HERMANN BREDEHORST—POLARIS (3)

Museum Makeovers

Curators abhor a vacuum: in the silent halls of royalty and the aging hulks of industry, they find new homes for art

MANY OF THE WORLD'S GREATEST ART MUSEUMS ARE squatters: they have taken up residence in buildings erected for entirely different purposes. The Louvre was the Paris home of France's Kings long before the Mona Lisa found a home there. Cosimo de Medici, the great Renaissance art patron, commissioned Giorgio Vasari to design the Uffizi Palace in Florence to provide grand municipal offices; centuries later, it became one of Italy's most visited museums. This mutation from patrician to public use serves history as well as art, for it has preserved many great structures of the past from destruction. Demonstrating why they are designers and not writers, architects call the makeover process "adaptive reuse," a stunningly flat phrase for such fascinating metamorphoses. In the past two centuries, adaptive reuse has traced the great currents of history, for art museums that once raced to fill the vacant palaces of royalty are now rushing to occupy the obsolete factories of industry.

The Hermitage Museum in St. Petersburg is centered around the czars' Winter Palace, which was completed in 1762. The regal structure presented a serious problem to the Bolsheviks, who seized power in Russia after World War I. As a symbol of royalty, it reeked of a class system that the communists had just overthrown. Yet as a symbol of Russia's cultural greatness, it could not be torn down or even ignored. The solution: it was preserved as a museum of fine art in newly christened Leningrad, where every comrade was welcome.

In the late 20th century, museum administrators turned to another source of space, finding inspiration in the vast, vacant buildings left behind as technological progress turned once bustling train terminals and factories into empty hulks, fodder for the wrecking ball. Shocked by the demolition of grand old buildings like New York City's Pennsylvania Station *(see page 125)*, historic preservationists and arts administrators teamed up to turn industrial-age ugly ducklings into information-age swans. In Paris, the Gare d'Orsay station was scheduled to be demolished in 1971; instead, it opened as the resplendent Musée d'Orsay in 1987 and is now one of the most visited museums in a city of museums. In 2000, the talk of London was the Tate Modern Museum, which opened in a former power station redesigned by the Swiss firm Herzog & de Meuron. In the U.S., the Dia Foundation in New York City craved a space large enough to hold the massive installations of such artists as Richard Serra and Walter De Maria. Its leaders found what they were looking for 90 miles north on the Hudson River, where a Nabisco factory in Beacon, N.Y., once produced food. Now it produces food for thought. ∎

The Prado

The Hermitage

CLOCKWISE FROM TOP LEFT: PATRICK WARD-CORBIS; FERDINANDO SCIANNA—MAGNUM PHOTOS; HARVEY LLOYD—GETTY IMAGES; LISE SARFATI—MAGNUM PHOTOS

The Prado

THE PRADO Construction began in 1785 on what was intended to be a center for natural-science studies, designed in a neoclassical style by Juan de Villanueva. After a war for independence from France intervened, the building was dedicated to the fine arts; it opened in 1819 as one of the world's first public museums

INTERIOR, THE PRADO One of the world's largest museums–a distinction it shares with the Louvre, the Hermitage and the Metropolitan Museum of Art in New York City—the Prado holds some 9,000 works. Its collections of Goya, El Greco and Velázquez are unmatched, and it has many Dutch and Flemish masterpieces

The Hermitage

INTERIOR, THE HERMITAGE Czar Nicholas I and his family occupied the building until 1904, when they sought refuge from Russia's revolutionary rumblings in the countryside. In 1917 the provisional government took up occupancy here; in 1919 the building became a museum

WINTER PALACE Begun by Empress Elizabeth, the building is the heart of the six-building Hermitage complex. It was designed by Italian architect Bartolomeo Rastrelli in a high-Baroque style and was completed in 1762. The main façade, above, is more than 600 ft. wide

Musée d'Orsay

Tate Modern

Tate Modern

The Prado

THE PRADO Construction began in 1785 on what was intended to be a center for natural-science studies, designed in a neoclassical style by Juan de Villanueva. After a war for independence from France intervened, the building was dedicated to the fine arts; it opened in 1819 as one of the world's first public museums

INTERIOR, THE PRADO One of the world's largest museums–a distinction it shares with the Louvre, the Hermitage and the Metropolitan Museum of Art in New York City—the Prado holds some 9,000 works. Its collections of Goya, El Greco and Velázquez are unmatched, and it has many Dutch and Flemish masterpieces

The Hermitage

INTERIOR, THE HERMITAGE Czar Nicholas I and his family occupied the building until 1904, when they sought refuge from Russia's revolutionary rumblings in the countryside. In 1917 the provisional government took up occupancy here; in 1919 the building became a museum

WINTER PALACE Begun by Empress Elizabeth, the building is the heart of the six-building Hermitage complex. It was designed by Italian architect Bartolomeo Rastrelli in a high-Baroque style and was completed in 1762. The main façade, above, is more than 600 ft. wide

Musée d'Orsay

Tate Modern

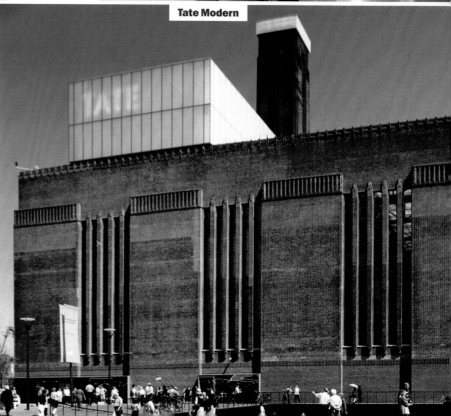

Tate Modern

Dia: Beacon

CLOCKWISE FROM TOP LEFT: MICHAEL S. LEWIS—CORBIS; AMY ETRA; PAWEL LIBERA—CORBIS; SCOT WARREN—AURORA PHOTOS

MUSEE D'ORSAY, PARIS, 1987 Designed by the respected architect Victor Laloux, the building opened as a train station in 1900. The barrel-vaulted central hall, once the teeming hub of the terminal, is 102 ft. high and 450 ft. long. In decline for decades, it was used as the shabby, forlorn backdrop for Orson Welles' 1963 film adaptation of Franz Kafka's *The Trial*

DIA: BEACON, UPSTATE NEW YORK, 2003 Project architect OpenOffice left ceilings and other portions of the building unfinished, exposing the innards of the former biscuit factory. Above, a viewer tilts to get a better gander at Richard Serra's 20-ton *Torqued Ellipses*, 1997

TATE MODERN, LONDON, 2000 The museum occupies a relatively recent structure, the Bankside Power Station, designed by Sir Giles Gilbert Scott and completed in two sections in 1947 and 1963. The building fell into disuse when the high price of oil made its operating costs inefficient. At far left is a 2003-04 installation in the great Turbine Room, *The Weather Project,* by Olafur Eliasson

111

Thinking out of the Box

His early work drew scorn (and bullets); now **Frank Gehry** creates
slippery masterpieces that make people fall in love with architecture

DON'T LET FRANK GEHRY CATCH YOU CALLING HIM
a deconstructivist or a populist or a post-Modernist or any of the other labels that have been
tacked onto his work. And don't try either the
characterization used since the beginning of his
career by some of Gehry's most fervent admirers—as well as
his most acerbic critics—that he is more an artist than an architect. "I don't call myself an artist," he insists. Instead, if you
must call him something, call Frank Gehry the world's most famous living architect. Even he couldn't argue with that.

Born Frank Goldberg in Toronto in 1929, Gehry grew up
playing in the back of his grandfather's hardware store, fashioning miniature cities from scrap pieces of lumber and wood
shavings. After moving to Los Angeles in the 1940s, the young
Gehry drove a truck while he attended art classes at night

school. He eventually
enrolled in the architecture program at the
University of Southern California and
changed his name to
Gehry, thinking that
his Jewish surname
might hurt his career
prospects. "It's not
something I would do
today," he says with a
hint of regret. "I'd like
to change it back."

After stints at Harvard's Graduate School of Design and a
year in Paris—during which he made pilgrimages to Europe's
architectural treasures—Gehry returned to Los Angeles and
began what promised to be an utterly conventional career, designing shopping malls and offices. On his own time, though,
Gehry began sketching out radically offbeat design ideas.

In the late 1970s, Gehry resolved to build one of these ideas:
he converted a Dutch Colonial bungalow he and his wife had
bought in Santa Monica into a wacky, off-kilter pastiche of raw
construction materials, parapets and exposed structural elements. Neighbors howled (and someone fired a bullet into the
house in apparent protest), but the architectural world was
put on notice: here was a major new talent of astonishing

originality. Not long after, an emboldened Gehry cut his staff
from 30 workers to three; struck up friendships with artists
like Robert Rauschenberg, Jasper Johns and Claes Oldenburg; and began a lifelong habit of drawing inspiration from
painting rather than from the work of other architects.

In the early 1980s, Gehry was commissioned to help Los
Angeles' Museum of Contemporary Art build a stopgap facility in an old police garage. Rather than disguise the existing
structure, he wrapped it in a canopy of steel-framed chain-link
fencing, setting up a fascinating tension between old and
new. Critics dubbed Gehry's style "car crash" architecture—
but as with a car crash, you couldn't look away.

In the late 1980s and early '90s, Gehry completed the Vitra
Design Museum in Germany, the American Center in Paris
and a retail center in Barcelona that contained a 90-ft.-high
golden fish. With these works, Gehry declared his independence from the angular, Euclidean design imperatives that
had dominated architecture for thousands of years, and he
embarked on an adventurous architecture of sweeping, sloping, curvilinear forms that had no precedent. Much of the
work was made possible by using innovative computer software originally developed for aerospace designers.

Then, in 1997, came Bilbao. For the Guggenheim Museum's new annex in a rusting Basque industrial city, Gehry created a sinuous, shimmering masterpiece, a titanium-clad
colossus that seemed a postcard from 2050—or beyond. In a
single swooping stroke, Gehry, long an architects' cult figure,
became a household name—at age 68. On a roll, the architect
followed Bilbao with undulating designs for the Experience
Music Project in Seattle and the Walt Disney Concert Hall in
Los Angles that wowed both critics and the public.

Gehry throws a welcome curve ball into our cityscapes of
Miesian rectangles. Modernism's glass-and-steel boxes were
well matched to the 20th century industrial economy. But as
factories yield to digits and the public square dissolves into the
borderless Internet, Gehry's forms speak to the ways in which
people and ideas circulate today. His funky materials and visual ruckus accord with the disorder of real life more closely
than the sharp-edged cartons of Modernism. It's too early to
tell whether his evanescent façades open a window into architecture's future or simply reflect a lone genius' quirky obsessions. But either way, the view is spectacular. ■

TIM STREET-PORTER—ESTO. INSET. JEFF FOLDBERG—ESTO

VERBATIM
"I want buildings that ... make people feel something, even if they get mad at them"
—Frank Gehry

Proposed Guggenheim Museum, New York City

PORTFOLIO: Frank Gehry

Norton Residence

Norton Residence

PROPOSED GUGGENHEIM MUSEUM, NEW YORK CITY Thrilled with the public response to Gehry's building in Bilbao, the Guggenheim Museum asked him to design a new museum to be located in downtown Manhattan. The result was this proposal for a massive arts complex, which will probably never be built, due to funding problems. The proposed building's main body would hover above the streetscape, allowing pedestrians uninterrupted views of the East River, while a promenade and extensive park space would provide an expansive new urban gathering place among the crowded streets of lower Manhattan.

NORTON RESIDENCE, VENICE, CALIFORNIA, 1982-84 "Buildings under construction look nicer than buildings finished," Gehry once said, and he set out to prove his point with a series of homes he built in Venice and Santa Monica, Calif.; they feature such unfinished materials as plywood, concrete block and chain-link fencing. The Norton Residence in Venice appears to be a deconstructed series of modules from the outside, but the interior offers a gracious, sweeping—and surprisingly homey—refuge from the world. The free-standing cubicle looks out on the Pacific Ocean; it's a witty nod to nearby lifeguard towers.

DISNEY CONCERT HALL, LOS ANGELES, 2003 Gehry began working on designs for a new home for the Los Angeles Philharmonic in the 1980s, but political and funding issues sidelined it for years. The building opened in the fall of 2003, to wide acclaim. Within the structure's slip-sliding-away exterior, Gehry created a warm, symmetrical interior in cozy Douglas fir, with gentle curves reminiscent of the work of Finnish architect Alvar Aalto; the floor is covered with a sizzling floral-pattern carpet that is a nod to Lillian Disney, Walt Disney's widow, whose $50 million gift sparked the project. "I didn't want to create a pseudo-classical hall for classical music," Gehry said. He succeeded.

❝ I'm interested in the game ... my clients have an object of desire in mind,

Disney Concert Hall

Guggenheim Museum, Bilbao

Disney Concert Hall

Experience Music Project

GUGGENHEIM MUSEUM, BILBAO, 1997 The titanium-clad structure is a slice of the future when seen from the centuries-old streets of Bilbao. The building now brings millions of visitors each year to the once neglected industrial city.

EXPERIENCE MUSIC PROJECT, SEATTLE, 2000 The architect claims the forms he used in this riotous, clashing museum of rock music were inspired by a heap of trash he found outside a guitar shop near his office in California.

GUGGENHEIM NYC MODEL: GAMMA; VENICE BEACH HOUSE EXTERIOR: ROGER RESSMEYER—CORBIS; INTERIOR: TIM STREET-PORTER—ESTO; DISNEY CONCERT HALL INTERIOR: TED SOQUI—CORBIS; EXTERIOR: NICK UT—AP/WIDE WORLD; BILBAO, SPAIN: JEFF GOLDBERG—ESTO; EXPERIENCE MUSEUM: POLARIS

and I try to realize it. I'm a geisha. ❞ —Frank Gehry

Where We Assemble

AFP—GETTY IMAGES

From pilgrimage sites to railroad and airline terminals, auditoriums and hotels, the architecture of assembly and transit creates unique buildings, where function often trumps form. While most buildings provide a longtime environment for a designated few, these buildings offer temporary shelter to the multitudes. They are studies in motion and multiplicity, in which the constant flow of thousands of people breeds vast size, surprising shapes and even, now and then, buildings that move those of us who only view them from a distance

GRAND MOSQUE MECCA, SAUDI ARABIA
Islam's most sacred site is crowded with pilgrims each year. The Ka'ba, a one-room black cube, is older than Muhammad

Athena's Sacred City

Towering over Athens, **the Acropolis** has felt the footsteps of Pericles, Socrates and Phidias, the founding fathers of Western civilization

ALL KINDS OF ENTERPRISES SHOULD BE CREATED which will provide an inspiration for every art and find employment for every hand," declared Pericles, the leading statesman of Athens, in the wake of the Greek city-state's triumph over the Persians at the Battle of Marathon in 490 B.C. Flush with victory, the Athenians resolved to undertake "such works as, by their completion, will bring everlasting glory." Before being driven off, the Persians had sacked Athens and destroyed the temples that sat atop its Acropolis ("high town"—a 10-acre mesa-like plateau that rises hundreds of feet over the surrounding city). This strategic vantage point had been used both as a fortification and a place of worship since Mycenaean times. And this was where Athenians would create the greatest of Greek public works projects and the high-water mark of architectural and sculptural achievement in the ancient world.

Pericles entrusted the design to his friend, the gifted sculptor Phidias, and two architects, Ictinus and Callicrates, who ordered that 20,000 tons of marble be quarried from nearby mountains. Ictinus was a master of entasis ("tension") and the optical tricks that cause right-angled buildings to appear top-heavy while making subtly curved structures seem both light in weight and straight of line. (Anyone who has stood at the base of a skyscraper and looked up has experienced this effect, as the building seems to lean out over the observer.) In truth, there are almost no straight lines in the entire complex of temples and shrines at the Acropolis—although nearly every line appears so. Perfectly vertical columns, for example, would look deceptively concave, seeming to lean outward. So Ictinus designed columns that bulge slightly in the middle and taper near the top, while leaning slightly inward. The effect is unique: an apparently flawless geometry that defies the gravity-bent, horizon-curved dictates of this world.

The centerpiece of the Acropolis is the Parthenon ("the virgin's place"), a temple in Doric style dedicated to the goddess Athena, the undefiled patron of the city. With the decline of the Greek Empire, history entrusted the Parthenon to a succession of caretakers. The Romans treated it reasonably well, and the temple served at different times as both a Christian church and a mosque. The Turks cared for it not very well—they used the Parthenon as a warehouse for explosives. The Venetians treated it worst of all—they bombed the Turks' ammunition dump while laying siege to Athens in 1687, setting off a huge explosion that wrecked the temple. The shattered ruin we see today is the product of man's hand, not nature's ravages: the Parthenon was preserved in almost its original form until the Venetian attack. In the 20th century, modern air pollution came to pose nearly as serious a threat to the remains of the Parthenon as did artillery in the 17th: the stone

VERBATIM
"The sun shines on it almost constantly, whatever the weather. It gleams gloriously."
—Gustave Flaubert

began to decay so rapidly that Greek authorities moved most of the remaining sculptural pieces indoors and replaced them with fiber-glass replicas.

Thievery also contributed to the Parthenon's ruination. Phidias' 40-ft. gold-and-ivory statue of Athena disappeared as Greece declined. Then, in 1802, a Turkish sultan issued a *firman* ("permit") for a British diplomat to make sketches and create molds of Parthenon sculptures. Lord Elgin interpreted this as license to cart off a shipload of priceless artifacts, which

SYLVAIN GRANDADAM— ROBERT HARDING

reside today in the British Museum, to the horror of Greeks.

Time has taken a grievous toll at the Acropolis, but it has spared enough of the Parthenon to provide proof, carved in stone, of the accomplishments of the Athenians. If Western civilization can be said to have a single birthplace, this is it. To stand on the Acropolis today is to gaze across not only the 25 miles that the view commands but also across the 25 centuries since Pericles and the Athenians sought—and earned—"everlasting glory." ■

CARRYING THE LOAD Seen from above, the Acropolis might be a boat plowing through a sprawling Athens. The south porch of the Erechtheion, the Temple of Athena Polias, is graced by a series of caryatids—female statues that bear the weight of the roof in place of columns. Those on the site are copies; the originals, to the dismay of many Greeks, remain with the Elgin Marbles in the British Museum

VERBATIM
Heroes have trod this spot—
'Tis on their dust you tread
—Lord Byron

H.H.—GETTY IMAGES

An Amphitheater to Die For

A geometry lesson in stone, the **Colosseum** marries one mighty ellipse to lofty walls borne by hundreds of arches—all to provide a view of a killing field

THE COLOSSEUM IN ROME WAS ERECTED ON THE EXACT site of Nero's Golden House, where the Roman emperor supposedly fiddled as he watched his city burn, in a fire he may have ordered set in A.D. 64. This great building was not only baptized in bloodshed: it was built for bloodletting, for here gladiators fought to the death. Begun by Nero's successor Vespasian in A.D. 71, it was completed by his son Titus nine years later.

The Colosseum is a triumph of design. The elliptical shape guarantees that every seat has good sight lines, while sturdy Roman arches support four mighty tiers, rising to 160 ft., that seated some 50,000 spectators. (The half-columns flanking the arches are mainly for show, not support.) Below the 290-ft. by 180-ft. floor of the arena, a maze of corridors and chambers held the essentials of the entertainment: dressing rooms for gladiators, cages for animals, storage rooms for stage machinery. Trapdoors allowed direct access to the floor of the arena, making for surprise entrances—and ensuring speedy removal of the dead and wounded.

Prototype for today's giant sports arenas, the Colosseum is kin to the great outdoor amphitheaters of the Greeks, where only symbolic blood was spilled; it is also the predecessor of the bull ring. While we think of such events as taking place under the direct glare of the sun, in its heyday the Colosseum was covered by an ingenious canvas awning that kept the sunshine and rain at bay. Its ruined state is not simply the work of time; it is the work of vandals—not the barbarian tribesmen Rome fought, but much later builders who plundered the structure for its limestone and marble. The process took centuries: Rome wasn't unbuilt in a day. ■

ASSEMBLE

Where a Ghost Plays Host

Ornate in every detail, the **Paris Opera House** is a gilded wedding cake of a building, yet it's most famous for something that isn't there: its phantom

COMPOSER CLAUDE DEBUSSY SAID IT REMINDED HIM of a Turkish bathhouse. The august London *Times* ventured that its architect, Charles Garnier, had perhaps "over-egged the pudding." Even Empress Eugénie, wife of its patron, upbraided Garnier: "What is this style? It isn't style. It's not Greek, not Louis XV, not Louis XVI." (His unfazed reply: "No. This is the style of the times. It is the style of Napoleon III, and you are complaining about yourself!") Call it what you will, in this case, nothing succeeds like excess: the Paris Opera House is the most famous auditorium in the world. Of course, it helps that this is a haunted house: the Palais Garnier will always be the home of novelist Gaston Leroux's Phantom of the Opera.

The Opera House is a lasting relic of a fleeting regime. It was commissioned by Napoleon III, the vainglorious nephew of Napoleon Bonaparte, who was eager to leave the stamp of his Second Empire on Paris. Garnier won an international contest to design the building in 1861, when he was only 32, but the elaborate structure wasn't completed until 1878, eight years after Napoleon III's fall. In its heyday, during Paris' Belle Epoque, Garnier's building well suited an audience that came as much to be seen as to see: its public spaces are nearly as extensive as its auditorium. The sumptuous grand marble staircase is made for sweeping ascents; the main foyer, above, like a stage, is surrounded by boxes to offer the best view of the fascinating events unfolding below. Pity the poor soprano who had to compete for the attention of these operagoers, reveling in the greatest show on earth: themselves. ∎

XAVIER ROSSI —GAMMA

CHANEY: BETTMANN CORBIS. MUSICAL: JOAN MARCUS

Is There a Phantom in the House?

E rik, the tragic hero of Gaston Leroux's 1911 novel *The Phantom of the Opera,* is an unforgettable character: a disfigured, yearning soul, he lives on an island on a lake beneath the bottom cellars of the Paris Opera House, swooning and brooding over the beautiful young soprano, Christine Daae. But even his creator might be surprised at the many lives his masked musician has led. Of some 18 film treatments, the most famous is a 1924 version starring Lon Chaney, above left. A master of macabre makeup, Chaney transformed Leroux's romantic figure into a horrifying, ghastly specter. In contrast, the hero of Andrew Lloyd Webber's 1986 musical-theater version is a deeply romantic paramour who seduces Christine (and audiences) from within the friendly confines of a sexy silver demi-mask.

The millions of tourists who visit the Opera House each year are often disappointed to find that the structure is not built over a lake or even, as many expect, a flowing river. A network of springs, however, does lie below it; before the foundations could be poured, water was pumped out of the site for months.

MARC SAYAG—PHOTOS12.COM—POLARIS

The auditorium was long home to both the Paris National Opera and the Paris Opera Ballet Company. But as the building aged, its flaws became evident: the auditorium offered too many partial-view seats, and by the 1980s both the interior and exterior of the building were shabby. In 1989 the Paris Opera moved to a new auditorium, the Opéra-Bastille, one of the *grands projets* commissioned by President François Mitterrand (I.M. Pei's glass pyramid at the Louvre Museum is another). In 1999 extensive renovations began on the Palais Garnier (as Parisians often call it). The main façade was entirely refinished by 2000, revealing the intense colors of its mosaics and marbles. The auditorium and stage were also overhauled, and many of the partial-view seats were removed. Restoration of the main lobby, side façades and other areas should be completed by 2007. And once again, opera is in the house: critics and audiences have never taken to the vast size of the Opéra-Bastille, and the National Opera now stages smaller productions in the reborn Palais Garnier.

CARDINALE STEPHANE—CORBIS SYGMA

RAZZLE-DAZZLE 'EM The façade is encrusted with ornament: six types of limestone; 10 variations of marble; mosaic panels edged in gold leaf; gilded statues. Inside, painter Marc Chagall's radiant 1964 mural on the interior of the dome is now a much loved feature of the building

A Majestic Portal Restored

In the exalting confines of **Grand Central Terminal,** a great temple of transit, rushing to catch your train may seem a labor worthy of Hercules

N THE 1930S, LISTENERS ACROSS AMERICA TUNED IN EACH Thursday night to the NBC Blue network, where, to the blare of locomotive whistles and screeching of steel wheels, an announcer breathlessly intoned, "Drawn by the magnetic force of the fantastic metropolis, day and night great trains rush toward ... Grand Central Station! Crossroads of a million lives! Gigantic stage on which are played a thousand dramas daily." The show got the name wrong: it's Grand Central Terminal—not Station, despite what everybody says— because rail lines begin and end there, rather than passing through. But the show got the glamour, drama, and sense of great doings exactly right. With its lofty barrel-vaulted concourse (275 ft. long, 120 ft. wide and 125 ft. high), massive cer-

emonial staircases and swank public areas, Grand Central seems to enlarge the life of everyone who passes through it.

A reluctant collaboration by two rival architectural firms, Warren & Wetmore and Root & Stem, the terminal is at once classical and innovative: the entire structure is built on piers several levels above its submerged tracks, whose excavation made room for New York City's great boulevard, Park Avenue. And the designers managed to make the building seem bigger inside than out by placing the floor level of its concourse at the bottom of the ceremonial stairs at each entrance, subtly submerging it below street level.

But by 1953, when NBC's "Grand Central Station" went off the air, both radio and the railroads were in decline. Grand

MELVIN LEVINE-GETTY IMAGES

ALFRED EISENSTAEDT-TIME LIFE PICTURES

A Majestic Portal Destroyed

The demolition of New York City's soaring Pennsylvania Station in 1964 to make way for a profoundly ordinary glass-and-steel office tower, in the basement of which the train station was stuffed, was simple vandalism. As the noted architectural historian Vincent Scully would later write, "One entered the city like a god … one scuttles in now like a rat."

Modeled on Rome's Baths of Caracalla, Penn Station's main entrance was adorned with a two-block-long row of Doric columns, each 35 ft. high and 4 ft. in diameter. All four entrances were crowned by a clock with a dial 7 ft. in diameter and flanked by statues of women symbolizing night and day. Inside, the waiting room was the size of the nave of St. Peter's Basilica, with Corinthian columns six stories tall and a vaulted ceiling 150 ft. high. Completed in 1910, the station was one of the defining structures of its age and the signature piece of designers McKim, Mead & White, then the leading practitioners of classical design in America.

But when the fortunes of the great railroads declined, the station's bankrupt owners quietly sold the edifice to developers, who tore it down and dumped the pieces in a New Jersey swamp. Public outrage led directly to the passage of the nation's first landmarks preservation law, which was quickly invoked to grant New York's other great station, Grand Central Terminal, protected status. Developers fought the law all the way to the U.S. Supreme Court, which in 1978 affirmed the authority of local governments to protect historic buildings. Plans are now under way to move rail operations from beneath the skyscraper into a refurbished McKim, Mead & White masterpiece, the monumental U.S. Post Office building across the street.

Central Terminal shared their fate, decaying into a tattered memory of itself. In the late 1960s it came within a hair's breadth of the wrecking ball; the enthusiasts who rallied to save it gave birth to America's historic preservation movement *(see sidebar)*.

In 1998 a $100 million refurbishing cleared World War II blackout paint from the terminal's windows, removed a huge billboard that had long blocked the sunlight and erased decades of grime from the ceilings, revealing a long-obscured mural of the night sky, complete with twinkling, lighted constellations. Redeemed, restored and resplendent, this space so central to the city is once again grand. ∎

BERTRAM BRANDT-BETTMANN CORBIS

Of Eagles and Grapefruit

Swooping down to earth to seize its prey—airline passengers—the daring
TWA Terminal evoked a graceful bird ... to everyone except its designer

FRESH FROM PRESIDING OVER THE 1957 DESIGN CONtest that awarded the commission for the Sydney Opera House to an unknown Joern Utzon, Finnish architect Eero Saarinen remained captivated by the young Dane's idea for cladding the structure in a series of segmented shells. At the time, Saarinen was looking for a visual theme to breathe life into an upcoming project of his own: the new terminal for Trans World Airlines at New York City's Idlewild Airport (now John F. Kennedy International Airport). But where Utzon found inspiration for his masterpiece in the curve of an orange peel, Saarinen took his cue from a somewhat different source. As his associate, Kevin Roche, would later recall, "Eero was eating breakfast one morning and was using the rind of his grapefruit to describe the terminal shell. He pushed down its center to mimic the depression that he desired, and the grapefruit bulged."

From these convexities, Saarinen took the idea for a soaring, arched roof that would trace the outline of a dome divided into four vaulting segments, each 50 ft. high and 315 ft. long. In his final design, each part of the dome touches the ground at only two points. But all four lobes converge at the navel of the terminal's roof (the point where Saarinen pressed down on his grapefruit) and lean against one another to form the third "leg" of support necessary for balance and stability.

From the moment the design was unveiled, critics and the public swooned, seeing the building as an architectonic metaphor for flight: the eagle-like silhouette of its entrance portal boasted a beak and talons, while its soaring rooflines mimicked wings in flight. Saarinen, for whatever reasons, professed to be shocked by the notion: "The fact that to some people it looked like a bird was really coincidental," he protested. "This was the last thing we ever thought about." A good try, but no sale: Saarinen later admitted that "the shapes were deliberately chosen in order to emphasize an upward-soaring quality of line. We wanted an uplift."

When the building opened in 1962, a popular backlash against the International Style had been gathering momentum for years. For many, Saarinen's playful, curvilinear creation offered a beautiful alternative to the harsh angularities of mainstream modernism. His design also reflected the boundless optimism of the early 1960s, a time when companies like TWA built for the ages: they sized up their trophy terminals the way Pharaohs eyed their pyramids. But if forward-looking in design, the TWA Terminal's smallish public areas looked backward to an era when air travel was for the privileged few, rather than the masses; it wore a tiara in an age of blue jeans.

A year before the project was finished, Eero Saarinen died of a brain tumor at only 51, leaving Roche and other partners to complete the TWA Terminal, along with several more of his signature designs: the St. Louis Gateway Arch, the main terminal at Dulles Airport in Washington and the CBS corporate headquarters building in New York City. Saarinen once reflected that the job of the architect was to place something "between earth and sky." With the TWA Terminal, he succeeded so completely that both the ground below and the air above seem improved by his mediation. ∎

EZRA STOLLER—ESTO

ANGELO HORNAK—CORBIS

DREAMS DEFERRED Inside, swooping curves convey a sense of fluid motion; a clock hangs where the vaults converge at the building's navel. The business assumptions on which the TWA Terminal was built began to shift shortly after it opened. The debut of larger jets, the explosion of air travel into a mass-market commodity and heightened security measures left the building overcrowded and undersized. The airline company struggled through several bankruptcies and was finally acquired by a competitor in 2001. The terminal building was saved in a 2003 agreement under which a new airline will use the space as a grand entrance foyer and ticketing center for a much larger terminal to be erected behind it

Sailing, Sailing

Over the ocean blue off the shore of Dubai rises a spell-binding homage to the humble dhow, the **Burj al-Arab Tower Hotel**

WHEN THE RULERS OF OIL-WEALTHY Dubai in the United Arab Emirates set out to turn their nation into a major tourist destination, they asked South African architect Tom Wills-Wright to create an icon—a building like the Sydney Opera House or Eiffel Tower that would bring worldwide attention to this land of only 700,000 people. Wills-Wright's Burj al-Arab (Arabian) Tower Hotel rose to the challenge. Built on an artificial island, it recalls the shape of the sail-powered dhows that have long plied these waters.

As of 2004, the Burj al-Arab is the world's tallest hotel, at just over 1,000 ft. But it's more than height that commands our attention: it's the building's bold engineering and its jaw-dropping bells and whistles, designed to provide envy-inducing talking points for the world's wealthiest travelers. Among them: the lily-pad heliport at top, which connects directly to a lavish penthouse, and an underwater restaurant, accessible only by submarine.

The building is braced against strong sea winds by a three-part exoskeleton, with a pair of tuning-fork masts on one side and a curving mast at the rear that takes the shape of a taut bowstring. Inside, a lofty atrium runs the full height of the structure. The beautiful red "sail" is more than a grace note: its Teflon-coated fiber-glass skin provides a screen from the withering sun, reducing heat and light in the interior, while it hides additional bracing. At night, the sail provides a backdrop for elaborate light shows—a reminder that Dubai is closer to Las Vegas than you might think. How much does it cost to stay here? If you have to ask, you probably won't be visiting. ∎

HODALIC–SAOLA–GAMMA

The Palladio of the Proboscis

Santiago Calatrava, an artist whose buildings often begin in sketches from nature, let his interest in organic forms run wild at the **Lyons Airport Railway Station**

COURTESY SANTIAGO CALATRAVA S.A.

YES, IT IS EXTRAVAGANT. YES IT BEGS FOR THE ATTENTION it receives. Yes, it "makes you look!" The railroad station at the Lyons Airport in France is one of the buildings dating to the 1990s with which the Spaniard Santiago Calatrava declared his intention of joining architecture's first rank of shapemakers. With its two mighty wings, the station is in part an homage to Finnish architect Eero Saarinen's birdlike TWA building at Kennedy International Airport in New York City *(see preceding page);* Calatrava frequently cites Saarinen as a key influence. But as for why a train station should resemble an insect—the dual arches that support the station's central "carapace" and wings strongly suggest a proboscis—well, that's Calatrava's secret. Surely this was one of the buildings curator Matilda McQuaid of the Museum of Modern Art had in mind when she wrote that Calatrava's work succeeds in "reaffirming a place for awe in the criteria for building."

Completed in 1994 at a cost of $200 million, the monumental station reflects its designer's intense interest in organic forms. Proud of his background in engineering, Calatrava once said, "Architects work in abstract terms, while engineers work more with models of nature." ■

VERBATIM
"Some architects conjure
unbuildable things ... [he] marries
beauty and pragmatism."
—Richard Lacayo

The Sculptor of Spaces

Enlivening Modernism's austere geometries with an artist's eye for natural forms, **Santiago Calatrava** creates a new poetry of the visual

LIKE HIS REVOLUTIONARY BUILD-ings—which manage to call to mind both the bleached bones of dinosaurs from the distant past and otherworldly edifices from the far-off future—Spanish architect Santiago Calatrava eludes labels. He is an architect above all, of course, but he is also a trained engineer, an urban planner and a gifted artist who often finds inspiration for his designs in his watercolors and sculptures. The fascinating thing about his work is that all his skills seem to be on display in every building he designs: the mind is engaged as abstract principles of physics take concrete form, even as the senses are wooed by the sheer, arresting beauty of his shapes, which often suggest natural forms: wings, praying hands, a mastodon's rib cage, an eyeball.

Calatrava's work makes familiar formulations—like the eternal tension between form and function—seem instantly dated, obsolete. Like Frank Gehry, he creates buildings whose "wow" factor makes people fall in love with architecture's possibilities—though Gehry often wraps the bones of his buildings in shiny wrappers, whereas Calatrava loves to expose them. And although the architect's best work to date has been done in Europe, Americans are increasingly waking up to the fact that one of history's master designers is in his prime and bearing gifts: in the years to come, Chicago and New York City will join Milwaukee, Wis., in harboring major structures by Calatrava.

Born in 1951 near Valencia, Calatrava was fascinated by design early on; he claims he is still inspired by the soaring Gothic columns of a mercantile exchange he visited as a boy. He earned a degree in architecture in Valencia but put off practicing to study civil engineering, receiving his doctorate in 1979. He didn't begin working as a designer until he was 30, but he soon won a reputation as a bridge builder: he has designed almost 50 bridges in various European countries. Typical of his audacious way with a span is the Alamillo Bridge (1992) across the Guadalquivir River in the southern Spanish city of Seville. The 820-ft. roadway does not rest on piers; instead, it is suspended, held by cables stretching out

from just one unstayed 466-ft. pylon, which leans back from the roadway at an angle of 58°—a hand grasping harp strings. Like much of Calatrava's work, the Alamillo Bridge can be traced to one of his sculptures, in this case a work he called *Running Torso*, a stack of marble cubes balanced by a taut wire.

From bridges, Calatrava soon graduated to transit stations: his train terminals in Lyons, France, and Lisbon manage to ennoble everyday commuting. His biggest project so far is for his native city: Valencia's $300 million City of Arts and Sciences is an enormous civic park that has reinvigorated the city's core. Its first building, opened in 1998, is an eye-shaped hemisphere set in a huge pond whose "pupil" is a planetarium, also containing an IMAX cinema and a laserium. In November 2000 the Science Museum opened (*above*), a building of white concrete and cascades of glass that from some angles conjures a dinosaur's spine caught in an ice floe. From another standpoint, it's a soaring forest of petrified trees.

Calatrava's debt to nature assumes even more palpable form when he treats his buildings as kinetic sculptures. A number of his bridges open up to allow ships to pass through them; the eye-shaped planetarium in Valencia sports a canopy that can be lowered like an eyelid. For a Roman Catholic cathedral proposed for Oakland (and now canceled) he designed a roof that opened and closed, suggesting two hands in prayer. His most prominent building in the U.S. to date also moves: the Milwaukee Art Museum entrance hall is topped with two giant "wings" that open up and flap in the wind, suggesting a gigantic bird or butterfly.

In January 2004, Calatrava showed off another strikingly kinetic building: a new transit hub to be built at ground zero in lower Manhattan. The terminal, featuring soaring 150-ft. white pylons and transparent glass walls, will be topped by a roof that will open with a hydraulic system to help cool it in the summer—and to allow a wedge of light to enter each year on Sept. 11. The movement, said Calatrava, signifies a phoenix rising from the ashes—an apt symbol, coming from architecture's foremost Renaissance man. ■

MITCH JENKINS; INSET: JOSE FUSTE RAGA—CORBIS

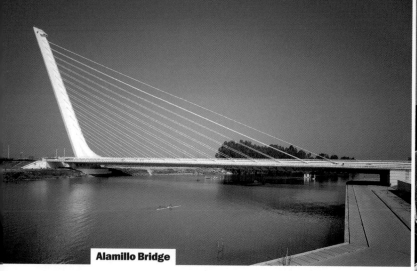

Alamillo Bridge

Oriente Train Station

City of Arts and Sciences

ALAMILLO BRIDGE, SEVILLE, 1992 By using a single pylon rather than two, Calatrava converts a simple span into a soaring essay in tension. The design, suggesting a lyre or harp, converts tensile strength from abstract theory into physical fact. Filled with concrete, the steel-cased pylon rises 466 ft. above the roadway.

ORIENTE TRAIN STATION, LISBON, 1998 The slender columns that support the folding geometric roof over the tracks resemble the fan vaulting of British perpendicular Gothic style—as do the lily pad columns of Frank Lloyd Wright's Johnson Wax Building. The camera's fish-eye lens slightly distorts the picture's perspective.

CITY OF ARTS AND SCIENCES, VALENCIA, 1998-Present This enormous project is opening in phases. The planetarium, top, resembles an eye, as does an arch of the Science Museum, bottom. An Opera House with three auditoriums for music is still to come.

PROPOSED TRANSIT HUB, NEW YORK CITY In January 2004, Calatrava unveiled his design for a new transit station that will arise at ground zero on the site of the former World Trade Center. The transparent entrance hall will bring natural light to platforms deep underground.

❝ My approach to sculpture and architecture is always watching the

Planetarium, City of Arts and Sciences

Milwaukee Art Museum

Proposed Transit Hub, World Trade Center

Milwaukee Art Museum

MILWAUKEE ART MUSEUM, 2003 Beam me up, Scotty! Calatrava's entrance building has been hailed as a masterpiece and denounced as a gimmick. Its 72 steel fins, painted white, unfurl (on a strict schedule) from a cone shape to create a *brise-soleil*, or sunshade, whose two wings flap in the breeze. The interior is equally futuristic. A successful flytrap for tourists, the entrance hall is all container and little content: it holds little art, following a recent trend in which museums commission trophy buildings that are destinations in themselves.

ALAMILLO BRIDGE: FERNANDO ALDA—CORBIS; LISBON TRAIN STATION: JOSE FUSTE RAGA—CORBIS; VALENCIA EXTERIOR: EDIFICE—CORBIS; VALENCIA INTERIOR: JOSE FUSTE RAGA—CORBIS; WTC PATH STATION PLANS: AP/WIDE WORLD; MILWAUKEE ART MUSEUM INTERIOR: JOSEPH SOHM—VISIONS OF AMERICA—CORBIS; MILWAUKEE ART MUSEUM EXTERIOR:JOSEPH SOHM—VISIONS OF AMERICA—CORBIS

behavior of the natural world. **"** —Santiago Calatrava

PETRONAS TOWERS, KUALA LUMPUR
The twin buildings in Malaysia's capital city, for a time the world's tallest, helped start a skyscraper boom in Asia

Where We Work

Suspended almost a quarter-mile above the ground, window cleaners in Malaysia prepare to start the day. Long ago, Gothic cathedrals soared into the sky to inspire souls longing to transcend the material world. Modern skyscrapers also seek height, but now the goal is to celebrate the material world—and our mastery of it

Rock of Ages

Not built, but carved, the **Treasury at Petra** keeps the secrets of a vanished culture

DEEP IN THE DESERT, THREE HOURS BY CAR from Amman, Jordan's capital city, stands all that remains of the great civilization of the Nabataeans—although stands may not be the right word for striking buildings hewed out of solid rock. We know the place by the name the Greeks gave it: Petra, Greek for stone. And certainly the Hellenic influence is present in the remarkable buildings at this site, of which the Treasury building, or Kaznah, at right, is the largest and most famous: its pediment and Corinthian columns are the unmistakable signature of the culture that built the Acropolis, although there are also Egyptian elements in the carvings on the façade. The name of the building is perhaps a misnomer; it may have been a royal tomb, perhaps holding a dead king's riches at one time.

Originally a nomadic Arab people, the Nabataeans settled in this region of wind- and water-carved canyons around the 6th century B.C. Through this canyon, the mile-long Sik, lengthy caravans passed, bearing pottery, silk and spices from China and India to Arabia and the Mediterranean. But the Nabataeans controlled the Sik, and they demanded tribute of all who passed through. In this "rose-red city, half as old as time," as the British Bible scholar and poet John W. Burgon once described it, the Nabataeans operated a business that Tony Soprano might understand.

But if the Nabataeans' wealth was ill-gotten, it was well spent. Work, work, work: they mastered hydraulic technology, channeling water through tunnels carved into the hills and along elaborate ceramic pipes to irrigate the land. They also excelled at pottery and metallurgy. By 100 B.C. the Nabataeans commanded a mighty empire of trade with outposts around the Mediterranean, and Petra was a flourishing capital that boasted an 8,000-seat theater, temples, proud villas and broad avenues, the remains of which can still be seen. Petra's wealth attracted the interest of the Romans, who became the first to conquer the city: the Emperor Trajan entered it in A.D. 106. The city continued to flourish under Roman rule, until an earthquake destroyed many of its buildings in A.D. 363; two centuries later, another earthquake led inhabitants to leave the city forever. Thinly re-settled in recent centuries, Petra was "lost" to Europeans until Swiss explorer Johann Burkhardt, disguised as a Muslim, managed to enter the city in 1812. ∎

ISRAEL TALBY—WOODFIN CAMP

VERBATIM
"Poised in wildness like a great carved opal glowing in a desert."
—Rose Macaulay

LOOK FAMILIAR? In the Middle Ages, European Crusaders built a small fort near Petra, a footnote to history that may have inspired filmmakers Steven Spielberg and George Lucas, who set the final scenes of *Indiana Jones and the Last Crusade* at the Treasury, left. The building probably dates to about 60 B.C.; its façade is 125 ft. high and 90 ft. wide. Inside is a large main chamber, with three smaller rooms branching off

OLD AND NEW
While the Galeria's vault was pioneering in its use of iron and glass, Mengoni's new buildings were copies of Baroque and Renaissance styles

STEPHANIE MAZE-CORBIS

Want to Sell? Cast a Spell

Milan's Galeria Vittorio Emanuele brought the outdoors in and created a refreshing new vision of urban life

IF SHOPPING MALLS AREN'T ENVIOUS OF SKYSCRAPERS, THEY should be. From humble beginnings, the skyscraper has grown steadily taller, more daring, more fascinating. But its contemporary, the shopping mall, has traced precisely the opposite trajectory: it's all been downhill since architect Giuseppi Mengoni brilliantly reimagined urban space with the Galeria Vittorio Emanuele, which opened in Milan in 1867.

To see the *Ur*-mall—the lofty prototype your local box of franchise joints utterly fails to live up to—take a stroll past Milan's great cathedral on your way to the legendary opera house, La Scala, and turn into the Galeria. Your heart will soar as your gaze travels upward ... and upward ... to meet the glass vault 120 ft. above that shelters you from the elements, as it casts a dim diurnal glow on the façades around you. Even bargain hunting seems noble in this palace of merchandising. While Mengoni's Galeria is not the first enclosed, pedestrian-only shopping mall in Europe—London and Paris had much smaller antecedents, and the St. Hubertus Royal Galleries in Brussels is perhaps its most direct ancestor—this great space was seen as revolutionary when it opened in 1867, and it remains one of the earth's most user-friendly urban environments.

Mengoni's great complex takes a cruciform shape, with the two short arms running 345 ft., and the longer arm 700 ft. The floors are mosaic tile; the image of a bull in the octagonal mosaic at the center of the space is an aphrodisiac—or so tourists are urged to believe. The first iron-and-glass gallery built in Europe, the space looks backward to the landmark 1851 Crystal Palace in London and forward to the 1889 Eiffel Tower and a host of great train stations. Big and bold in outlook, it is charged with the fresh energy of its time, when Italy's long-squabbling republics began to unite and a new dawn for the nation was at hand. Sadly, the architect did not live to see that dawn, or even to accept congratulations on his great work: two days before the Galeria opened, he slipped and fell to his death from atop one of the buildings under his vault. ∎

THE SHINING
Chrysler, an engineer, and Van Alen chose Nirosta steel, a special alloy that catches and reflects light, for the building's spire

BETTMANN—CORBIS

OSCAR GRAUBNER—TIME LIFE PICTURES

OUT ON A LIMB Walter Chrysler hired Margaret Bourke-White, a 23-year-old whose pictures of factories had made a splash in Henry Luce's new business magazine, FORTUNE, to photograph his prized building. "Art that springs from industry should have real flesh and blood, because industry itself is the vital force of this great age," she once wrote, in what sounds like an Art Deco manifesto. Here she perches on one of the giant steel-coated eagle gargoyles at the spire's base

WORK

Pushing Sci-Fi into the Sky

The Roaring Twenties became the Soaring Twenties in a flashy Art Deco masterpiece, William van Alen's over-the-top **Chrysler Building**

LIKE THE SOARING GOTHIC CATHEDRALS OF THE MIDDLE Ages, skyscrapers are exercises in exuberance and up-lift, optimism frozen in girders and glass. No building better captures the pure look-at-me exhilaration of the form than the needle-nosed number William van Alen de-signed for auto magnate Walter Chrysler in 1930. It's the Buck Rogers top that we can't see enough of: a cascade of Art Deco arches urged upward by giant, spiky triangular windows, it seems to be perpetually unfolding, organic and alive. But the rest of the building is just as daring, for Van Alen, who had studied in Paris as a winner of a scholarship sponsored by the American Society of Beaux Arts Architects, adorned it with a hodgepodge of automotive-age details that somehow work: giant eagle gargoyles (modeled on Chrysler hood ornaments), a frieze of oversized hubcaps, abstract motorcars. The lobby

murals feature airplanes and Detroit assembly lines—Art Deco's love affair with machines. Alive with the feel of its time, Van Alen's work shows up such Gothic Revival towers as Man-hattan's Woolworth Building (1913) and Chicago's Tribune Tower (1925) as second-hand knockoffs, stylistic dead ends.

Sadly, Walter Chrysler's interest in the building centered on its short-lived title as the world's tallest; once it was overpow-ered by its crosstown rival, the Empire State Building, he quarreled with Van Alen, refused to pay his fee and ended up litigating with the architect. And that's too bad, because in this great structure Chrysler scrawled his name indelibly on Man-hattan's skyline. "The age demanded an image/ Of its accel-erated grimace," Ezra Pound wrote about the irrational exu-berance of the times. Van Alen's Chrysler Building makes the velocity vertical and turns the grimace into a grin. ∎

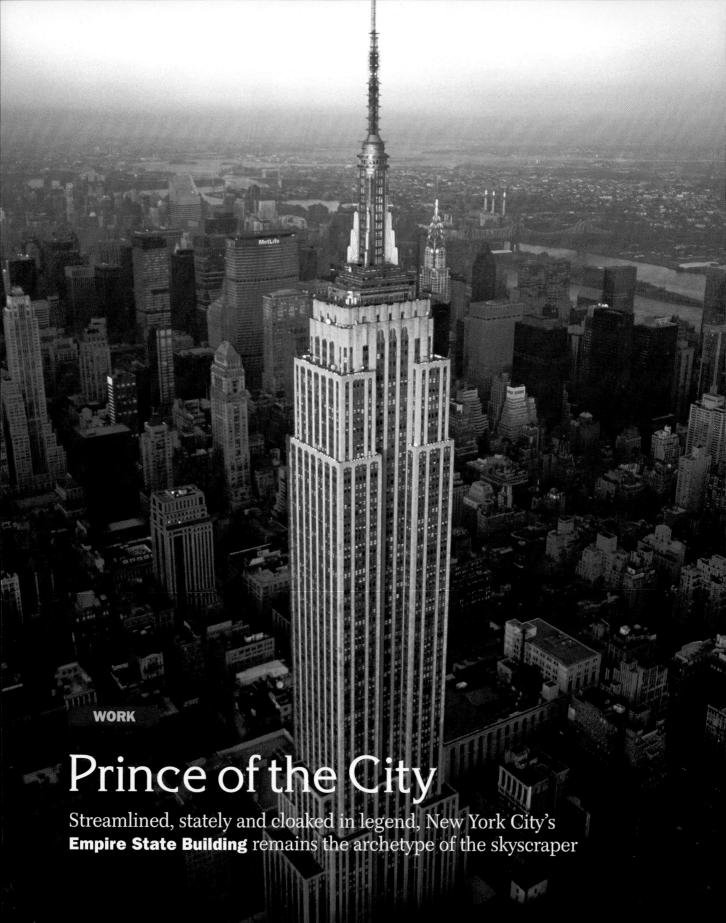

Prince of the City

Streamlined, stately and cloaked in legend, New York City's
Empire State Building remains the archetype of the skyscraper

CONCEIVED IN COMPETITION, BAPTIZED IN BALLYHOO and calibrated for comparison, the Empire State Building is dedicated to the proposition that all skyscrapers are not created equal. This most emblematic of urban structures was the winner of a frantic race to the sky, as developers and architects vied to capture the title of world's tallest building. The contest was a final frantic spasm of jazz-age optimism before the stock-market crash of 1929—but so strong was the impetus behind the Empire State Building (and so deep were the pockets of its builders) that riveters kept joining its girders even as sightings of scaffolding grew scarce in Manhattan's streets. The long years of economic woe and the great labors of World War II ensured that no rival would top its 1,250-ft. height for decades. The Twin Towers of the World Trade Center finally stole the building's thunder in 1971, and Chicago's Sears Tower soon topped them. No matter. When we think of skyscrapers, this is it—the icon.

Fueled by new media, including radio, newsreel films and mass magazines like TIME, the 1920s were a Barnumesque era of publicity stunts, gaudy spectacles and giddy excess. In the world of business and real estate, the age's Olympian impulses—swifter, higher, stronger—saw tycoons trying to top one another by constructing ever taller edifices. In Manhattan, the year 1928 saw two moguls—automaker Walter Chrysler, TIME's Man of the Year, and Wall Street wunderkind George Ohrstrom, a multi-millionaire at only 33—locked in a battle to erect the world's tallest building. As Neal Bascomb tells the story in his engaging account *Higher* (Doubleday; 2003), Chrysler and architect William van Alen won the contest by hiding the spire of their building until it was almost completed, then erecting it by surprise. But their glee was short-lived, for both Ohrstrom's 40 Wall Street and the Chrysler Building were soon dwarfed by a late entry, the Empire State Building. Designed by architect William Lamb, it was the brainchild of Chrysler's rival, John J. Raskob, creator of General Motors.

The astute Raskob engaged former New York State Governor and failed presidential candidate Al Smith to be the front man for the big tower. The Happy Warrior was good copy: his gift of gab, political pull and sheer ebullience put the massive project on the front pages of newspapers across the country day after day. As a result, the Empire State Building was a legend even before it was completed in 1931.

In the years that followed, the lore of the building only grew. Hollywood immortalized it as a jungle-gym for the giant ape King Kong in the classic 1933 movie. On July 28, 1945, 13 people died after a B-25 bomber pilot, lost in fog, rammed his plane into the building's 78th floor. In 1961 control of the building was acquired by real estate maven Harry Helmsley, whose wife and partner Leona was later branded the "Queen of Mean" by tabloid papers for her imperious ways. Whatever their flaws, the Helmsleys gave the building new luster in the 1970s by illuminating its top with colored lights at night; the hues change to celebrate holidays, seasons, visitors to the city, even winning sports teams. Kitschy? Yes—but somehow the colors seem a fitting crown for this monarch of buildings.

On the morning of Sept. 11, 2001, workers on the upper floors of the structure were startled to hear a passenger jet roaring downtown along the Hudson River at low altitude and top speed: hours later, the Empire State Building was once again the tallest skyscraper in Manhattan. This time around, it was a distinction smothered in sorrow. ■

YANN ARTHUS-BERTRAND—CORBIS

The Secret: Skeletons of Steel

BETTMANN CORBIS (X2)

A worker "rides the ball" in the picture above, as the Empire State Building takes shape. Behind him is the just-finished spire of the Chrysler Building, which would soon be dwarfed by its cross-town rival. The big steel girders visible in both pictures are one of the essential ingredients—another is the elevator—that make skyscrapers possible. Prior to the 1870s, buildings could not rise much higher than five stories, for the load-bearing masonry walls on their lower floors grew ever thicker to support the weight of the floors above them. In his 10-story Home Insurance Building in Chicago (1879), architect William LeBaron Jenney, supposedly inspired by the design of a bird cage in his home, introduced the use of a cagelike steel skeleton to bear the main weight of the building. Freed of shouldering the load of upper floors, masonry walls could now be made much thinner, for they were a mere "curtain" hung over the steel support frame.

The Empire State Building arose with startling speed even as the U.S. economy crashed around it. On its site at 34th Street and Fifth Avenue in Manhattan a beloved building, the original Waldorf-Astoria Hotel, had stood since 1893. The hotel was demolished, and work began on the Empire State Building's foundation in late March 1930. Incredibly, it was completed and dedicated on May 1, 1931—a marvel of planning and efficiency that still impresses today's builders.

FACT
In the late 1960s, five streets were
erased to make way for the Trade Center's
16-acre superblock

Gone but Not Forgotten

Arrogant and aloof, the Twin Towers of the **World Trade Center** captured
New York City's swagger and sent it skyward—for fewer than 30 years

THEY BECAME THE WORLD'S TALLEST TWINS BY ACCIdent. When the Port Authority of New York and New Jersey set out to build the World Trade Center in the late 1960s, plans called for 10 million sq. ft. of office space, which could have been spread across the 16-acre site in lower Manhattan in any number of ways. But after a public relations person blithely suggested that the project might be designed to create the loftiest skyscraper in the world, the "biggest" bug took hold. One tower became two when architect Minoru Yamasaki decided that a pair of slender columns thrusting skyward would be less oppressive than a single, stout massif. Yamasaki, an advocate of "a friendly, more gentle kind of building," had made his reputation with office towers that wove strands of concrete and steel into complex, delicate surfaces that looked very much like textiles. And the Twin Towers would be no exception: their narrow columns and vertical stripes of glass, set back in shadow, would give them the appearance of being clad in pinstripes.

Inspired by sources as diverse as the Doge's Palace in Venice (its romantic motif of arches culminating in columns shaped the towers' ground floors) and the Katsura Palace in Kyoto (whose slender bamboo fence was echoed in the slim vertical lines that reached a quarter-mile into the clouds), Yamasaki labored mightily to create giants that were still human in scale. But when they were finally completed in 1971, the minimalist style and maximalist size of the big twins made them hard to love—and the failure to incorporate the towers and their huge plaza into the street grid of lower Manhattan made them seem isolated, overbearing intruders rather than friendly neighbors. Even the bragging rights were fleeting: in 1974 Chicago's Sears Tower surpassed the twins in height by less than 100 ft.

New Yorkers loved to grouse that the unadorned behemoths looked like the boxes that the Empire State Building and Chrysler Building came wrapped in. But just as the Eiffel Tower grew on Parisians who initially hated it, New Yorkers came to take a grudging pride in the silvery tuning fork that anchored their skyline. The towers were at their best in the evening: transformed into pillars of light, they rose as icons of optimism and power, fitting companions to America's nearby beacon of freedom, the Statue of Liberty. As the song says, "Don't it always seem to go/ That you don't know what you've got till it's gone?" ∎

LOOKING UP After the Twin Towers were destroyed on Sept. 11, 2001, architect Daniel Libeskind won an international competition to create a new World Trade Center to arise at ground zero. His plan calls for a series of buildings, the tallest of which, Freedom Tower, above, will rise to 1,776 ft.

This picture of the Twin Towers was taken in 1977. In later years, Battery Park City was built on 23 acres of landfill created when the Trade Center site was excavated; the development obscured the harbor view of the towers' lower floors

BILL PIERCE—TIME LIFE PICTURES—GETTY IMAGES

DEBOX INC—AP/WIDE WORLD

VERBATIM
"It's like modern art or modern music.
It takes time to get used to it."
—Michaeld Sandberg,
bank president, 1986

To Rework The Workplace

With his innovative **Hong Kong & Shanghai Bank Tower,** Britain's Norman Foster cracked open the dull skyscraper and let in the sunshine

A T FIRST GLANCE, THE BUILDINGS OF ONETIME PART-ners Norman Foster and Richard Rogers seem to be all about their surfaces: their inside-out, high-tech designs transform boring infrastructures into witty façades. But beyond exulting in gizmos, their designs reflect deep thinking about the way buildings work and the way people work within them. When Foster won a 1979 contest to design the headquarters of the Hong Kong & Shanghai Bank Corp. in Hong Kong, he reimagined the skyscraper from the ground up: how it supports itself; how light enters the building; how workers move around within it; even what they see, for he managed to turn every office into a room with a view.

Foster sought to open up the building, so it wouldn't be a confining stack of vertical boxes. Rather than support his floors by channeling their weight downward, Foster hung modular office blocks from giant, inverted V-shaped trusses, visible on the façade. The trusses, in turn, are supported by enormous "masts" at the ends of the building: the engineering is similar to the way a roadway hangs from the pillars of a suspension bridge. Service elements such as elevators and heating ducts are housed in the end masts. In most office buildings, valuable space at the center of each floor is set aside for these core services, but the interiors of this building are open, creating a sense of enormous spaciousness. Freed of supporting columns and the need to hide service cores, many floors are designed on the open plan.

Seeking to divide the building into "villages," Foster's elevators stop only every five floors. To move between nearby floors, workers ride one of 162 escalators, completely visible and humming with movement: this place is a beehive of activity. On the lower floors a 10-story atrium makes a grandly imposing entry hall; on weekends, when most office towers are locked and dark, its ground-floor plaza is a lively gathering place for locals. On the roof, the mirrors of Foster's trademark "sunscoops" funnel natural sunlight throughout the building.

The downside: some workers want more privacy, and construction of the building ran way over budget. But this is a structure of vast imagination and daring—and perhaps the tintype of office buildings of the future. ∎

MIKE YAMASHITA—WOODFIN CAMP (2)

SHEDDING LIGHT: A 10-story atrium, above, creates a spectacular entry space for the building; outside, inverted V-shaped trusses resist typhoon winds. At left, Foster's building faces the historic British Governor's Residence. At the rear is I.M. Pei's multifaceted Bank of China Tower (1990)

Malaysia's Mirror Monsters

Claes Oldenburg's binoculars? Not even close: the twin **Petronas Towers**
in Kuala Lumpur are proud to be the world's…uh…second-tallest buildings

WHEN IT COMES TO SKYSCRAPERS, SIZE MATTERS:
the more flights, the more bragging rights. Since
their first appearance in Chicago in the 1870s,
the big spires have flourished on the generous
fertilizer spread by glory-seeking architects, tycoons with edifice complexes and civic boosters frantic to top the next town's
tower, if only by a smidgen. This recipe created America's big
skyscrapers, and it's the force powering the most recent wave
of colossal buildings, centered in Southeast Asia and China.
Case in point: the Petronas Towers in Kuala Lumpur, Malaysia. In the unlikely event that they should ever find themselves
adjacent to the building whose crown as tallest they stole in
1997, Chicago's Sears Tower, the two 1,476-ft. spires would loom
over the former champ by a commanding … 22 ft.

Designed by esteemed architect Cesar Pelli, the matching
monsters reach 88 stories, are capped by 246-ft. tapered pin-

BIG STORY An extensive mall sits between the towers, offering
1.5 million sq. ft. of space for retail and entertainment use,
including a theater, a petroleum exhibit (Petronas is the national
oil company of Malaysia) and a parking facility. The diameter of
each tower's central core is only 150 ft., while the circular
design maximizes window space. Inside, the Billionaire's Club
restaurant (no millionaires allowed?) swoops in an elegant swirl

nacles in classic Malaysian style and are connected by a 160-
ft. skybridge. But alas, Petronas Towers: your elevator shafts
may be long, but your reign was short. By 2004, Taipei 101, a
1,667-ft. behemoth in Taiwan's capital, had snatched the title
of world's tallest tower. And Daniel Libeskind says his 1,776-
ft. Freedom Tower, slated to rise in lower Manhattan, will be
taller still. If an institution is the lengthened shadow of one
man, skyscrapers are the lengthened shadow of their builders'
egos. And when it comes to builders' egos, size matters. ■

AVENTURIER PATRICK—GAMMA (2)

VERBATIM
"We never set out to design the world's tallest building ... but we started thinking, Why not?" —John Pickard, Pelli design team leader

VERBATIM
"The tower is no longer
an isolated form ... it addresses itself
to the context of the city."
—A. James Speyer

Master of the Modern

Refining buildings to their essentials, Ludwig Mies van der Rohe found God in the details and unlikely poetry in rigorous geometric forms

FRANK SCHERSCHEL—TIME LIFE PICTURES. INSET: MARK KAUFMAN—TIME LIFE PICTURES

ONCE LAUDED AS THE PARENT and patron saint of Modernist architecture, he would later be damned as the man who turned cityscapes into drafty canyons lined by banal boxes—mean, cheap abstractions of glass and steel. In truth, Ludwig Mies van der Rohe was neither angel nor devil. Rather, he was a stonemason's son from the German countryside who never lost his love for purity in materials, strength in expression and clarity in design.

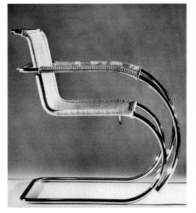

Born in Aachen in 1886, Mies apprenticed to the influential German designer Peter Behrens. Influenced by religious thinkers like Augustine and Aquinas who emphasized intellectual rigor, he became obsessed with stripping away the ornamentation ("macaroni" he called it) he found in most European architecture. He was not above personal artifice, however; he added his mother's maiden name, van der Rohe, to his own, which is German slang for "lousy."

Although he was reluctantly designing neo-Georgian houses for clients as late as 1924, Mies first gained worldwide attention for his "honest" architecture with his German Pavilion at the Barcelona Exhibition in 1928. In this cool, confident temple, slender chrome-plated columns supported a thin, hovering roof slab and surrounded an open-plan interior divided by movable glass panels. The building converted an entire generation of young architects to Mies' clear-eyed vision of the future; sadly, it was demolished at the exhibition's end.

Mies' career almost followed suit. After Adolf Hitler took power in 1933, the reductive classicism favored by the Nazis became Germany's official style, a point underscored when the Nazis shut down the famed Bauhaus design school, where Mies had succeeded Walter Gropius as director. Encouraged by American acolytes of his emerging "International Style," Mies emigrated to the U.S. in 1938. Nine years later, when young architect Philip Johnson organized a show of the German's work at New York's Museum of Modern Art, Mies was all but officially anointed the high priest of contemporary architecture. A series of massive masterpieces followed: the campus of the Illinois Institute of Technology, twin apartment towers on Chicago's Lake Shore Drive and, most memorably, the Seagram Building in New York. Each featured what Mies called "universal space" interiors: vast, vertical open-plan expanses that could serve any purpose, anywhere in the world. In each of them, structure became ornament: Mies exposed supporting girders that traditional architects had always hidden. By distilling buildings to their essential elements—vertical and horizontal planes, bare but lustrous materials—Mies created a rigorous new poetry of form. "God is in the details," he liked to say.

The bronze-and-glass Seagram Building (1958), Mies' masterpiece, secured his position as the pre-eminent form giver of 20th century architects. Raised above street level on a block-long pink-granite platform, the elegant tower is set back on the site and framed by a broad plaza with reflecting pools. When first built, its luminous façade glowed against the masonry-clad buildings around it like a messenger from the future.

Yet the Seagram Building also contained the seeds of a backlash against Mies and Modernism. Just as many writers have found the lean prose of Ernest Hemingway easy to imitate but impossible to duplicate, lesser architects began aping Mies' spare, geometric style—while missing his numinous details. Developers urged them on, for a skyscraper devoid of embellishment is a thing of beauty when viewed from the bottom line. The result was a generation of wretched buildings perpetrated in Mies' name—boring boxes that made Modernism a synonym for the banal.

Mies died in 1969, the same year that American architect Robert Venturi published an influential rejection of less-is-more Modernism, punning that "less is a bore." But with the passage of time, the works of the master are increasingly standing out from his imitators. The austere German's reputation is rising from the ashes, and it isn't alone: in 1987, Mies' great lost masterpiece, the German Pavilion for the Barcelona Exhibition, was rebuilt on its original site. ∎

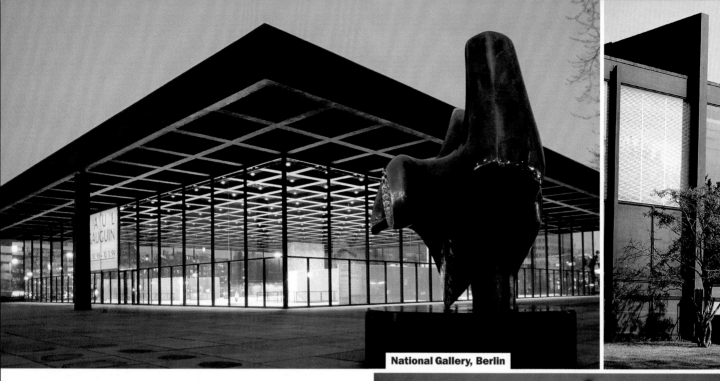

National Gallery, Berlin

PORTFOLIO: Ludwig Mies van der Rohe

Chapel, Illinois Institute of Technology

Tugendhat House

NATIONAL GALLERY, BERLIN, 1968 The skillful use of glass gives Mies' buildings transparency and clarity. In the daytime, glass brings outdoor elements into the interiors of his buildings; in the nighttime, the illuminated structures become containers of light, glowing with beauty. Here, the main galleries are underground, below the terrace; temporary exhibits are within the pavilion.

CHAPEL, ILLINOIS INSTITUTE OF TECHNOLOGY, 1953 The sanctuary becomes a jewel box of light in this deceptively simple chapel, which blooms when the interior is illuminated. Mies designed 10 buildings at the Chicago university, extending the Windy City's reputation as a cradle for innovative architecture, which it first won in the late 1800s.

TUGENDHAT HOUSE, CZECH REPUBLIC, 1930 Today, this interior looks almost generic: it could be the dining room of any modern home—and that's a tribute to the pervasive influence of Mies' stripped-down aesthetic. When the Tugendhat House was first built, its spare look was utterly revolutionary. The architect's signature chairs were innovative in both design and technology; it took years to perfect the resilient stainless steel that supports the seat.

❝ Less is more. ❞—Mies van der Rohe

Crown Hall, Illinois Institute of Technology

German Pavilion

Seagram Building

CROWN HALL, ILLINOIS INSTITUTE OF TECHNOLOGY, 1956 The flat roof of the building is not supported from below; it is suspended from eight gigantic exterior steel columns, two of which can be seen framing the entrance in this picture.

GERMAN PAVILION, BARCELONA EXPOSITION 1928 The walls disappear in Mies' groundbreaking building, obliterating the distinction between inside and out. Mies used the finest materials; imitators copied his geometry, minus the richness of detail.

SEAGRAM BUILDING, 1958 The building's front plaza is unfinished in this picture, which shows the key features of the design: exposed structural elements, glass façade, a transparent first floor over which the main edifice seems to float. When safety codes mandated that the building's structural steel girders be encased in concrete, Mies designed a second set of steel members to hang outside them, thus "revealing" the structural forms within. The architect's love of order sometimes gave way to a mania for control: he lost the battle to control every window shade in the building from a single switch.

BERLIN NATIONAL GALLERY: MARTIN KIRCHNER/LAIS—AURORA PHOTOS; TUGENDHAT HOUSE: ROBERTO SCHEZEN—ESTO; ILLINOIS TECH CHAPEL: FRANK SCHERSCHEL—TIME LIFE PICTURES; CROWN HALL AT ILLINOIS TECH: G.E. KIDDER SMITH—CORBIS; SEAGRAM BUILDING: BETTMANN CORBIS; BARCELONA PAVILION: SCOTT FRANCIS—ESTO

" Less is a bore. " —Robert Venturi

Buildings That Surprise Us

"STILTSVILLE" HOUSE
MIAMI
Once fishing shacks and restaurants, these
Biscayne Bay structures are now homes. Some
27 stood in 1960; only seven remain

A Parthenon on pilings, this residence in the "Stiltsville" area south of Miami offers a perfect study in the eternal waltz of form and function: its all-important purpose—keeping its head above water—has the upper hand over its unadorned exterior. In this chapter, we take a detour from presenting single great buildings to explore structures that are unique, either in the purpose they serve, the materials from which they are constructed or the fanciful forms they assume

Crystal Palace

Winter Garden

ABOVE: NO CREDIT. RIGHT: TIMOTHY HURSLEY

Glass Class

Looking at London's Crystal Palace, architects saw clear into the future

WHEN JOSEPH PAXTON'S REVOLUTIONARY CRYSTAL Palace opened as the home of London's Great Exhibition of 1851, it created an uproar. Critics denounced it as little more than an overgrown greenhouse—or compared it to plumbing. But the new building won far more admirers than detractors: dappled with light and shadow, uplifting visitors with its vast vaulted concourse, this showplace of glass was an inspiring, ennobling space. And it was more: this was the first great building of the Industrial Age, a structure that pointed the way toward the future, as it demonstrated that the era's new materials—plate glass and iron—could create exciting new shapes that captured the energy of the times in physical form.

The building was assembled from prefabricated units and erected in only three months by semi-skilled workers. Although it was designed to be disassembled after the two-year exhibition, the building was so beloved that it was moved to a park in south London, where it stood for many years before it was destroyed by fire in 1936. (The building's portability was further proof of its utter technological novelty.) With its curtain walls of iron and glass, the building is the direct predecessor of the modern skyscraper and of other breathtaking buildings of glass, from train depots to homes to chapels. ■

WINTER GARDEN, BATTERY PARK CITY, 1988 A glass vault in the shape of a cornucopia covers the centerpiece of a retail gallery at Battery Park City in Manhattan. Severely damaged in the 9/11 terrorist attacks, it reopened on Sept. 17, 2002

Lloyds of London

Glass House

Thorncrown Chapel

CLOCKWISE FROM ABOVE: STUART FRANKLIN—MAGNUM PHOTOS;
THOMAS ENGLAND; EZRA STOLLER—ESTO

CRYSTAL PALACE, LONDON, 1851 British architect Joseph Paxton was a former gardener who learned the secrets of iron-and-glass construction in building palm courts and lily houses. The walls and roof of the building were constructed from 293,000 sheets of plate glass

GLASS HOUSE, CONNECTICUT, 1949 American architect Philip Johnson, a disciple of Ludwig Mies van der Rohe's and a leading figure of both modern and postmodern design, built this see-through retreat in 1949, using the same open-plan interior as Mies' Farnsworth House

LLOYDS OF LONDON, 1985 Richard Rogers brought the flair for spectacle he showed off at the Pompidou Centre in Paris to the London headquarters of one of the world's most staid firms. The gallery of the Briton's building tips its hat to Paxton's talismanic Crystal Palace

THORNCROWN CHAPEL, ARKANSAS, 1980 Architect Fay Jones, a disciple of Frank Lloyd Wright's, designed this graceful chapel to blend into the forested bluffs of the Ozark Mountains in northern Arkansas. The 48-ft.-high building is covered by more than 6,000 sq. ft. of glass

SHERRLYN BORKGREN—AURORA

"Fairy Chimneys," Turkey

KAREN HUNT—CORBIS

SURPRISE

Stonewalled

We're used to seeing native stone employed in home construction, but these unique buildings really rock

SPRINKLED ALONG THE GÖREME VALLEY IN CENTRAL Turkey is a series of cone-shaped lava mounds the locals call "fairy chimneys." The locals also call these unusual natural formations home, for they and their forefathers have carved living spaces out of the lava spires for hundreds of years. The cones are made of two forms of lava: a softer, earlier form, tufa, was covered by a harder form; when the tufa is removed, living space is revealed.

Among the world's most fascinating places of worship are 12 churches in Ethiopia built by Coptic rulers of the Zagwe dynasty. Some of the churches are caves that have been expanded by excavation, but the most fascinating of them are carved out of solid bedrock and are surrounded by trenches that allow visibility and access. Inside, the churches glow with bright mosaics. And for sheer oddity, consider the troglodytes of Coober Pedy, Australia, who avoid the burning Outback sun in homes hewn into abandoned opal mines. ■

Coober Pedy, Australia

DIRCK HALSTEAD—LIAISON—GETTY IMAGES

"FAIRY CHIMNEYS," TURKEY The cone-shaped structures are made of hardened lava from which softer lava has eroded or been dug out; they are found in a triangle roughly five miles on a side in central Turkey, in historic Cappadocia. In addition to serving as dwellings, the "fairy chimneys" are also used as churches. Below left, stone streets connect the lava formations into villages

COOBER PEDY, AUSTRALIA Want to "build" a new home in this underground town in the Outback, located in used-up opal mines? It will take a boring machine about a day to dig out your four-bedroom home. Some 70% of residents live beneath the ground here, where the mercury stays cool as the summer heat bakes those aboveground. At top right is the Weathermill family in their living room and kitchen; at right is a bookstore

BET GIORGIS CHURCH, ETHIOPIA, circa A.D. 1200 The Coptic rulers of the Zagwe dynasty oversaw a high point of culture in Ethiopia. Under the most powerful of them, King Lalibela, 12 great churches were created. Some were made by hollowing out caves; others, like cruciform-shaped Bet Giorgis, were hewn out of solid bedrock

KAL MILLER—WOODFIN CAMP

SIMON GROSSET—SPOONER—GAMMA

Bet Giorgis Church, Ethiopia

Here Today, Gone Tomorrow

In most cultures the home is an emblem of stability, a still point in a turning world. But for the planet's few remaining nomads, home is a moveable feast

DESIGNERS WRESTLE WITH BLUEPRINTS TO ACHIEVE A wide variety of goals: loftiness, size, comfort, thrift, majesty, efficiency. But portability is seldom among them. One exception, Joseph Paxton's great Crystal Palace, was a prefabricated structure that was assembled in only three months in 1851, then disassembled and rebuilt elsewhere. Moshe Safdie's Habitat apartment complex is not mobile, but its modular design was intended to launch a new era of more mobile construction, in which precast concrete units could be easily moved and assembled on-site to provide inexpensive housing in growing cities. But Habitat did not lead to the revolution Safdie hoped for.

To find buildings that are truly portable, we must turn to the world's nomads, whose building forms are a kind of folk technology developed over countless generations. The structural apparatus of such buildings is generally taken from the tent: an infrastructure of wooden poles or lathes is covered by skins or canvas to create a dry shelter from rain and wind.

The sublime exception to this rule is the igloo of ice constructed by the Inuit people of the Arctic Circle, which achieves a kind of perfection in both its shape and its materials. Like all domes, it is the most efficient way to provide shelter, and its essential materials, snow and ice, are abundantly available for free. It is one of mankind's most efficient buildings. ∎

JERI GLEITER—GETTY IMAGES

Iranian *Chambareh*

RAD ESLAMI—GAMMA

IGLOO, CANADA The Inuit (or Eskimo) igloo at left costs nothing, aside from labor, to construct. Made of snow packed into cubes, it is reinforced on the inside as the heat of a fire melts the inner walls to form a solid shield of ice, sealing any chinks in the walls and helping retain interior heat

CHAMBAREH, IRAN The Shâhsavan (also known as Ilsovan) nomads of Iran erect dome-shaped yurts, *chambareh,* that can be taken down and put up in less than an hour. Beneath the hide covering is a skeleton of bow-shaped sticks that converge at the top center and slot into a circular ring. The *chambareh* lacks the lower wooden rim employed by some Iranian nomads, as well as by Mongols

GER, MONGOLIA Like the Iranian nomads, nomad Mongols erect different types of portable homes, or yurts. The most elaborate and widely used of them is the *ger,* which, like the Iranian *oy,* features a lower rim with a wood lattice that elevates the ceiling inside. Most *gers* have post-and-lintel doorways, limiting their portability

NATIVE AMERICAN TEEPEE, DAKOTA TERRITORY, 1880 The classic American teepee maximizes floor space by combining a pyramid shape with a tent-style support system whose masts are tree branches stripped and lashed together. Simpler than the *ger,* the teepee is thus much more portable

KRZYSZTOF WOJCIK—GAMMA

Mongolian *Ger*

CORBIS

Native American Teepee

Olympic Park, Munich

BETTMANN CORBIS

Suspending Your Disbelief

When an ancient form meets modern materials, interest in tents is intense

EASY TO ASSEMBLE, EFFICIENT IN FUNCTION AND BASED on materials that are widely available in nature, the tent is one of mankind's oldest, humblest structures. Most tents, like the Native American teepee or Mongolian *ger,* are composed of an exterior of cloth or hide that covers an interior framework. But when 20th century architects set out to reinvent the tent using advanced synthetic materials, they turned to a slightly more sophisticated form, in which the roof of the structure is held up by wires attached to tall supporting masts. The engineering is similar to that of a suspension bridge.

The suspension format is an efficient way to shelter a large area, so it's not surprising that its most interesting applications have come at large sporting venues. One of the first such structures to attract international interest was the Yoyogi National Sports Center in Tokyo, which was the primary setting for the 1964 Olympic Games. Japanese architect Kenzo Tange, a student of the Swiss-French master of concrete construction,

Le Corbusier, hung the roof of the large arena from two tall supporting masts at either end of the building. Suspending the roof of the structure not only provides for a welcome lightness in the interior but also eliminates the need for supporting columns, thus ensuring that sight lines for each of its 15,000 seats are unobscured. The roof consists of two equal segments, one per side; a central skylight allows natural light to enter the arena.

German architect Otto Frei, who had long been interested in the tent form, demonstrated its unique capabilities memorably at the 1972 Munich Games. Frei suspended multiple roofs over the entire Olympic complex, including the semicircular arena. The covering offers spectators basic shelter from sun and rain, but it is distinguished by its beauty as well as its utility. Made of PVC-coated polyester fabric, the roof is light in feeling, alive with circulating breezes, while it is also beautifully luminous, a dappled scrim between spectator and sky through which clouds can be seen. No wonder architects' interest in tents is looking up.   ∎

Olympic Stadium, Munich

MUNICH OLYMPIC STADIUM, 1972
Though spectator stands completely surround the elliptical main arena, Frei's translucent roof, right (also visible from the outside in the picture at left), covers only the half of the stadium most exposed to direct sunlight

YOYOGI NATIONAL SPORTS CENTER, TOKYO, 1964 Suspending his twin roofs from masts, Kenzo Tange created swooping, organic forms that are demonstrations of tensile strength in action. Like the roofs, the central support structure descends in the middle between the two main masts at either end of the building

RINGLING BROTHERS CIRCUS TENT, 1956 The tent was long associated with the itinerant circus form. The legendary Big Top used by the Ringling Bros. and Barnum & Bailey Circus was large enough to shelter three performance rings and 16,000 spectators. Elephants were harnessed to help hoist the four main supporting masts into position. Below, the last time the Ringling Bros. Circus performed under its big canopy was at an appearance outside Pittsburgh, Pa., in 1956

Yoyogi Center

Ringling Bros. Circus

DAVID CANNON—ALLSPORT—GETTY IMAGES

ANGELO HORNAK—CORBIS

IAN WALTON—GETTY IMAGES

Be It Ever So Humble …

There's no place like a second home that follows you
around, a hotel made of ice or an arboreal retreat

WE CAN'T TELL YOU WHAT THE HOME OF THE FUTURE will look like, but we're prepared to wager it probably won't bear any resemblance to the sci-fi saucer below, which was designed by Finnish architect Matti Suuronen and marketed in the 1960s in two versions, Futuro I and Futuro II. Made of reinforced plastic and originally envisioned to be used as ski cabins, the homes were manufactured and sold in kit form through such sources as *The Whole Earth Catalog*.

The Futuro's nifty circular floor plan includes a central fireplace (with space for a stereo conveniently located beneath the hearth) and streamlined seats that convert into beds. And when it's time to come down to earth: "Deploy the retractable stairs!" The legs are adjustable, permitting the home to remain level on sloping terrain. About 20 of the houses are still believed to be in use around the world.

Perhaps even more unusual than the Futuro house is a hotel made of ice. But when the Hotel Glace (Ice Hotel) opened its doors outside Quebec City in the winter of 2000, it was an immediate hit. The hotel features walls of snow that are 4-ft. thick and steady interior temperatures between 23° and 28° F. One of the most frequently asked questions on the Ice Hotel website: What about rest rooms? Potential visitors are advised that an adjacent heated facility will accommodate their needs.

Two more novelties round out our survey of defiantly different vacation domiciles. The first is a brilliant exercise in streamlining, the Airstream "Clipper" mobile home, the brainchild of onetime advertising copywriter Wally Byam, which first went on sale in 1936. The second is a retreat in the treetops, a shady bower for whiling away an idle hour. ∎

BETTMANN CORBIS

FUTURO II, 1968 The prefabricated home was made of reinforced plastic; it sold with a complete interior for $14,000. When the worldwide oil crisis struck in the early 1970s, plastic prices soared, making production costs prohibitive

Ice Hotel

THIS PAGE, CLOCKWISE FROM TOP LEFT: LAYNE KENNEDY—CORBIS; SCOTT T. SMITH—CORBIS; PEGGY MALONE

ICE HOTEL, QUEBEC Everything in the hotel—columns, floors, ceilings, beds, tables, barstools and the registration counter—is made of ice. In 2004, there were 31 rooms and 10 suites. Two art galleries and a movie theater are on the premises, and should things heat up, there's also an all-ice wedding chapel

TREEHOUSE RESORT, OREGON The Out 'n' About "treesort" is one of a number of bed-and-breakfasts worldwide that offer cabins in the trees. Visitors to the Oregon establishment can choose from 18 cabins, from 8 to 52 ft. above ground. Kids play on swinging bridges, rope ladders and a ropes course

AIRSTREAM TRAILERS Wally Byam, Airstream's founder, was a visionary who incorporated aircraft design—a riveted aluminum exterior and streamlined styling—into his travel trailer. The original 1936 Clipper sold for $1,200. Enthusiasts continue to converge at remote sites to swap tales of life on the road

Treehouse Resort

Airstream Trailers

Form 10, Function 0

Think of it as architecture à la WYSIWYG: what you see is what you get. And why shouldn't a hot-dog stand look like a weenie, if it helps catch your eye?

YES, THERE IS A FORMAL ACADEMIC TERM FOR THE SORT of kitschy commercial structure whose appearance apes what it sells: it's called programmatic architecture. Whether zoomorphic, anthropomorphic or weeniemorphic, such quaint architecture-as-advertising structures once played a far more prominent role on America's highways. The few survivors, formerly the bane of the design community, are now just as likely to be embraced for their unassuming, Pop Art tackiness.

Over the decades, such nutty roadside attractions can accumulate a rich patina of lore. Consider Lucy, the Margate Elephant, which was built in 1881 as a tourist attraction by real estate developer James Lafferty but whose 123-year history traces the larger story of its location. Designed to publicize a new real estate development in South Atlantic City (later Margate), the viewing platform thrived as the Jersey Shore became a major fun spot but fell into disrepair as the city's for-

tunes declined after the Depression. Along the way, the big pachyderm, which is made of wood covered in tin, weathered two hurricanes and was even used briefly as a house. Always a favorite of children, who love to clamber up the stairs in its legs to the viewing platform in its howdah, the structure was embraced by preservationists when it faced demolition in the early 1970s. Lucy was moved to a new location and her exterior was lovingly restored in 1974 ; she was officially registered as a National Historic Landmark in 1978. In the latest stage of Lucy's long journey, her long-neglected interior was restored and opened to the public in 2003.

Lest you think there's no future for such overdesigned publicity stunts, well, consider the Burj al-Arab Hotel, shaped like a giant dhow *(see page 128).* Or take a drive to Newark, Ohio, and take a gander at the Longaberger basket company's home office, a $30 million, seven-story building in the shape of, yes, a great big basket, with two big handles on top. Sweet! ■

MARGATE ELEPHANT, NEW JERSEY, 1881
Lucy has been offering visitors to the Jersey Shore a view of the goings-on from the howdah on its back for 123 years. In the 1970s a "Save Lucy" committee raised the money to preserve and restore the elephant, which tops out at 65 ft.

BETTMANN CORBIS

Tail o' the Pup

THIS PAGE, CLOCKWISE FROM TOP LEFT: CRAIG AURNESS—CORBIS; JOHN MARGOLIES—ESTO (3)

TAIL O' THE PUP, LOS ANGELES, 1945 Reminder of a bygone era in Southern California when you could have a drink at the Brown Derby (shaped like a brown derby), Tail o' the Pup was almost torn down in the 1980s but still puts on the dog near its original location. It has been featured in several movies

HAINES SHOE BUILDING, HELLAM, PA., 1948 This "really big shoe" is 25 ft. high, 48 ft. long and 17 ft. wide; it has three bedrooms, two baths, a kitchen and living room. Built by local shoemaker Mahlon Haines, it has been a guesthouse and ice-cream stand and is now a museum

DONUT HOLE, LOS ANGELES, 1968 Last survivor of an original batch of five such shops, the Donut Hole's twin semi-toruses are 26 ft. high and constructed of fiber glass

SALVADOR'S, SOUTH DARTMOUTH, MASS., 1935 Still open and still dishing out ice cream (with jimmies), the big milk jug is a much-loved summer destination

Haines Shoe Building

The Donut Hole

Salvador's